We Are Born with the Songs Inside Us

We Are Born with the Songs Inside Us

Lives and Stories of First Nations People in British Columbia

Katherine Palmer Gordon

Harbour Publishing

Harbour Publishing Co. Ltd.
P.O. Box 219, Madeira Park, BC, V0N 2H0
www.harbourpublishing.com

Cover photograph: *Stutsun Transforming* by John Marston, photo by
   Jeff Weddell Photography, courtesy Inuit Gallery of Vancouver
Edited by Cheryl Cohen
Index by Stephen Ullstrom
Cover and text design by Roger Handling, Terra Firma Digital Arts
All photographs copyright the photographer
Printed and bound in Canada

Harbour Publishing acknowledges financial support from the Government of Canada through the Canada Book Fund and the Canada Council for the Arts, and from the Province of British Columbia through the BC Arts Council and the Book Publishing Tax Credit.

Library and Archives Canada Cataloguing in Publication Data Available

ISBN 978-1-55017-618-6

Dedication

The following people would like to dedicate their stories as indicated:

Evan Adams: To my parents, Leslie and Mary Jane Adams

Merle Alexander: To my mother, Stella Alexander, and my grandmother, Viola Hopkins

Kim Baird: To my daughters, Amy, Sophia and Naomi

Tewanee Joseph: To my wife, Rae-Ann Joseph

Peter Leech: To my late father, Walter Gregory Pascal Leech

John Marston: To my family and friends

Lyana Patrick: To my family, past, present and future: Mussi!

Troy Sebastian: To my mother, Patricia, who deserves all the credit for the person I am today, especially my strident desire for social justice and peace

Anne Tenning: To my mother, Elizabeth Tenning

Trudy Warner: To my son, Jaden; the philosophy "Life is full of choices" is one I hope he learns early in life

Lisa Webster-Gibson: To everyone with two skins to fill

Penny White: To my late father, Willard White

Bill Yoachim: To my Auntie Vi, the late Chief Viola Wyse

For my part, I wish to dedicate this work to everyone in it, and to friendship, goodwill, respect and song—*KPG*

Contents

Foreword: Shawn A-in-chut Atleo   8

Introduction   10

1. You Are Who You Are: Lisa Webster-Gibson   17

2. One Hundred Percent Me: John Marston   30

3. Travels Across the Medicine Line: Lyana Patrick   42

Thoughts from Puuglas (Jody Wilson-Raybould)   54

4. First-Class Citizen: Gino Odjick   55

5. First, I Say My Name Is Peter: Peter Leech   65

Thoughts from Bruce Underwood   79

6. The Good Life: Penny White   80

7. Just Doing It: Tewanee Joseph   91

Thoughts from Clarence Louie   103

8. Standing on Our Own Two Feet: Kim Baird   104

    What's in the Tsawwassen Treaty   118

9. We Will Go Forward: William Yoachim   121

10. Aiming Past the Finish Line: Beverley O'Neil   131

11. On the Battle Line: Merle Alexander   145

Thoughts from Shawn A-in-chut Atleo   159

12. A Matter of Choice: Trudy Warner   160

   A Short History of the Maa-nulth Treaty   170

13. Born to Be Free: Evan Touchie   174

Thoughts from Bonnie Leonard   180

14. Only One Lifetime: Troy Sebastian   181

15. Weathering All Storms: Anne Tenning   194

Thoughts from Adam Olsen   206

**16. Working Really Hard Just to Get to
   a Normal Place:** Evan Adams   207

Thoughts from Sophie Pierre   222

Postscript: The Strength of Identity—

   Connections between Culture and Well-being   225

Acknowledgements   237

Index   241

About the Author   247

Foreword

On June 11, 2008, the prime minister of Canada offered an apology on behalf of all Canadians to the people who had lived through the terrible era of the Indian residential-school system. My late grandmother, Elsie Robinson, was sitting with me as we listened to him speak. She turned to me and said: "Grandson, they are finally beginning to see us."

I have worked toward the goal of reconciliation between Canada and First Nations all of my adult life. As my friend Peter Leech says in "First, I Say My Name Is Peter,"[1] to achieve that goal, it's first important to accept the fact that we are all simply just human beings. I agree. I believe that seeing us as human beings, as people with our own unique perspectives and lives, is a fundamental first step toward understanding who we are, rejecting false and imposed stereotypes, and ultimately reaching reconciliation.

The fact is that there *is* no one stereotype or archetype that can be labelled as being First Nation or Indigenous. That is too simplistic by far. Likewise, ideological, black-and-white thinking has no place in reaching understanding and acceptance. Finding genuine common ground requires first seeing, then listening to one another's stories, and hearing each other's unique voices, thoughts and perspectives. That is how we end up really "seeing" each other as vibrant, beautiful human beings, with different and shared cultures that are living, growing and constantly evolving. This is the essence of achieving recognition of our peoples as individuals *and* as nations with rights, responsibilities and a key role to play in mutual partnership with all of Canada.

The people whose stories are told in this book represent a rich spectrum of individuals whose lives and work are worthy of not only understanding, but celebration. As author Katherine Palmer Gordon indicates in her "Introduction," *We Are Born with the Songs Inside Us* could have included thousands of people. Canada

1 Page 65

is incredibly fortunate: First Nations make up the fastest-growing population in the country. There are thousands upon thousands of young First Nations people growing up today who, together with the kind of individuals whose stories are told in this book, represent a future for this country that is brighter than it has been for a long, long time.

I am always so proud to introduce Canadians and others around the world to the First Nations peoples of Canada: to our heritage, our culture and our lives. I am equally pleased to introduce *We Are Born with the Songs Inside Us.* We need these stories to be told, read and celebrated.

Thankfully, after a rich and challenging life of constant struggle and determination, my grandmother witnessed this country starting to see us. Today we carry on her work and that of so many others who went before us in leadership and strength, to protect our ways, to honour our responsibilities and to affirm and respect our peoples, our Nations and our future. It is my hope that, through sharing our stories, through reaching out for respect and understanding, one day my own grandchildren will know greater understanding and respect. Perhaps they will turn to their grandchildren and say: "They see us now finally and now we work together in respect and harmony for our shared responsibilities."

Shawn A-in-chut Atleo
National Chief,
Assembly of First Nations
March 26, 2013

Courtesy Assembly of First Nations

Introduction

One evening a few years ago, I went to listen to a presentation about bird calls by Salt Spring Island naturalist John Neville. Neville described all birds as being "born with a song inside them." But for that song to emerge in its full beauty and range, as the expression by that individual creature of the unique melody that belongs to its particular species— a song that will protect it, will attract its mate to it, will communicate alarm and hunger and satisfaction and joy—is anything but automatic.

Young birds must learn their unique songs from their fathers, Neville explained. A baby bird that does not have the opportunity to hear its father sing will never learn its proper song. It will remain bereft of its complete identity and the single most important characteristic governing its ability to take care of itself, be independent, communicate and relate—not only to members of its own species, but to all other creatures.

It's an apt analogy in the context of the many First Nations people in Canada who never have had the chance to learn their songs from their parents. Some were sent to residential schools, where their mother tongue was beaten out of them. Some were taken from their homes by government agencies determined to eradicate their culture. Some lost their parents to the twin twentieth-century demons of addictions and disease, or they escaped, taking to the streets. In turn, they had children to whom they could not teach songs they had never learned themselves. Many of them struggled to live to their full potential.

This sad story is something with which Canadians have become increasingly familiar in recent years, through the media and as a result of the efforts of bodies such as the Truth and Reconciliation Commission, created in 2009 to help raise public awareness of the legacy of the residential-school system. Deprive people of their language, history, community and traditions, as the residential schools did, and—as the First Nations of Canada understand all too well—they will suffer an inevitable and tragic decline in both their cultural health and their well-being as a whole.

But there is a much happier story here also: that of all the First Nations men and women across the country who were fortunate enough to learn their songs at their parents' feet. Some are reconnecting to their roots and learning their songs as adults. Others, drawing upon what is inside them and what they know about themselves, are simply creating their own unique melodies. Thus armed with the essential components of a healthy life—confidence in cultural identity, language, traditions and related contemporary practices—children, adults and elders alike are thriving in every aspect of their daily lives, whether it be education, careers, family and community life or sports and the arts. They are determining their path in life with self-assurance and pride.

That is not despite being steeped in their culture, as stereotypes would suggest, but *because* of it. They are empowered to give expression to the songs inside them, the cultural voices within them with which they were born and which they have learned to use every day in compelling and meaningful ways, both as First Nations people and in their own individual and unique ways.

This simple but fundamental truth has profound implications for Canadian society. First Nations are the fastest-growing segment of the country's population. That's hugely exciting for anyone who understands the great potential that statistic holds. Increasing numbers of young people of Aboriginal heritage in Canada—proud of their identity and culture, confident in their abilities and strengths, full of joy and humour and promise— are emerging in the forefront of business, government, the arts, social and environmental stewardship, technology and sports. They are tackling education, community well-being and parenthood head-on and successfully. Many are—or will be—widely acknowledged and respected and loved for their achievements, large and small.

This book shares and celebrates the stories of some First Nations women and men you may never have heard of before, as well as some who are household names in British Columbia. Some live on Indian reserves, some don't. Many of them are learning or relearning their languages. They are moving forward with pride, courage and strength to do remarkable things. They are going to school, learning technical skills, studying art and filmmaking and engineering and medicine and law. They are playing professional hockey and leading their communities. They are looking after old people, and working for city hall. They love to golf, run triathlons, play in bands, do stand-up comedy, hang out at the park, and watch their favourite television shows with their kids. What they all have in common is an unshakeable belief in the importance of their cultural heritage to their well-being, their success at what they do, and their everyday lives.

Their stories are stories of hope and inspiration, not only for other First Nations people, but for all Canadians. You may not recognize them as they walk down the street. They don't have "Aboriginal" stamped on their foreheads. They are our neighbours, friends, the people next to you in the grocery store line-up, coaching your kids' soccer or rowing team, doing cancer fundraisers, driving ambulances and fire trucks, and acting as role models and mentors for those wanting to follow in their footsteps.

They are living their lives like other Canadians, but their cultural heritage, so intrinsic to their identity and connections, also underpins their daily existence. They all have a keen awareness of the tragic history their parents and cousins have suffered, the legacy of colonization and the residential schools, the loss and the problems and the isolation, the fear and the anger. That legacy affects them too.

Despite that, all these people are leading successful, inspirational lives, confident in their cultural and human identity. Those who are very well known include Ahousaht's Shawn A-in-chut Atleo, the head of the national Assembly of First Nations. There's also former chief Kim Baird, who in 2008 brought home the first modern urban treaty in British Columbia for the Tsawwassen people in Vancouver. Evan Adams is a celebrated movie and television actor. Gino Odjick came to Vancouver two decades ago, from the tiny Quebec community of Kitigan Zibi, to make his name as a National Hockey League player. Famous or otherwise, all of them were born with their songs inside them, and all of them have shared their stories here with grace, simplicity and complete candour.

It was tempting to include many more individuals than the ones illustrating these pages. As it was, each person I spoke to provided me with dozens more names of other people I could have interviewed. It was incredibly difficult to include just a few representative people. In addition to the stories that are in the book, I have included a handful of compelling thoughts on culture, identity and the future for First Nations children that were offered to me in conversations I had with several prominent First Nations women and men over the past few years. But if this book included the full story of every smart, articulate, self-confident, inspirational, ordinary yet wonderful young First Nations individual in British Columbia, let alone Canada, it would be thousands of pages long (and that would just be Volume 1).

I've made that comment to many people now, some of whom thought I was exaggerating. I'm not. I could have included Carey Price, for example, goalie for the Montreal Habs National Hockey League team, who hails from Ulkatcho First Nation. I could have shared Michele Guerin's story: lawyer, mother, grandmother, former commercial fisherwoman and one-time aspiring police officer, this remarkable Musqueam woman spent several years as director of research for the National Centre for First Nations Governance before co-founding her own law partnership, Guerin Tetrault & Associates, in Vancouver. Many young First Nations men and women become lawyers these days; as Merle Alexander points out in "On the Battle Line" (page 145), it's a logical career choice for young Aboriginal people—like Douglas White (Snuneymuxw First Nation) or Merv Child (Dzawada'enuxw)—wanting to do something to help protect the rights of their communities, elders and future generations.

I could have written about twenty-two-year-old Tyrone Sylvester of Cowichan Tribes, who won four gold medals in canoeing at the 2006 North American Indigenous Games in Denver, Colorado, or young Nisga'a business leader Art Mercer, helping his remote northern community manage its extensive asset portfolio. What about Ktunaxa Nation youth Marisa Phillips, pioneering First Nations language revitalization through podcasting technology, or Nanaimo's Rob Ellis, a young Métis man who started his own excavation company at the age of nineteen and six years later, in 2010, won an Aboriginal Business Award from the British Columbia Achievement Foundation?

You're getting the picture, I'm sure. But please be patient, because I want to throw in a few more names anyway. Nikki Stewart, a twenty-nine-year-old Tr'ondëk Hwëchin (Yukon Territory) woman has built a life for herself with her husband, Aron, on Gabriola Island, caring for a household of animals that she adores, baking endless cookies and cakes to give away to her friends, and riding her bike to her job at a local store. Nikki has faced some really tough times in her short life, but despite that, in this small community she's generally described by people who know her as "that girl who *always* has a huge smile on her face." Nikki has been getting to know her northern family better in recent years, and her smile has grown even bigger as a result.

There's Charlie Gillis from Nuu-chan-nulth territory, self-taught carpenter and besotted father of three-year-old Tehya, who as I type is building a new deck at the house next door. Maxine Tanner is a Wet'suwet'en woman from near Burns Lake in northern British Columbia, who has lived in Nanaimo and worked for the municipality there most of her adult life. She's one of those brave souls you see paddling in a dragon boat on Nanaimo Harbour every week, rain or shine, relishing every moment. Like Nikki, she has been proudly learning more about her origins as an adult, but with the excitement and pleasure of a child discovering wonderful new experiences. Max is one of the most remarkable, warm-hearted, down-to-earth and beautiful people I know.

I could have written about Candace Campo, founder of a successful kayaking business in Sechelt, on the Sunshine Coast; or Cheryl Bryce, Lekwungen (Songhees), who works tirelessly to protect the traditional lands of her people and to ensure that British Columbia's wild foods, like camas, don't disappear.

There's the high school band in the remote village of Lax Kw'alaams, north of Prince Rupert, who played "O Canada" to a group of business people visiting from Vancouver, with more heart than any of us had ever heard, as the fog rolled in over a small fleet of fishing boats tied up nearby and the cluster of neat, small, colourful homes that comprise the tiny port community. The intense frowns of concentration on the kids' faces were replaced by huge smiles of relief when they were done, and the audience clapped and whistled and stomped their feet on the floor in appreciation of their efforts.

Teyem Thomas, Snuneymuxw, who answers the telephone when you call the Vancouver office of the Assembly of First Nations, is a typical young small-town girl loving every minute of her recent move to the big city from Nanaimo. Doug Neasloss, wildlife photographer and guide, is one of the youngest chiefs of the Kitasoo/Xai'xais and a clear-eyed visionary for his community. Marven Robinson, spirit bear guide and expert, is one of many Gitga'at people from the beautiful little community of Hartley Bay who braved a dark night and the cold seas north of Kitimat back in 2006 to rescue the survivors of the sinking *Queen of the North* and bring them all home to look after and comfort them.

It really is tempting to keep going. But as I've already admitted, it is way too long a list, so I'll stop. The point is that there really are literally thousands upon thousands of creative, energetic, ordinary and extraordinary and inspirational people in this country who happen to be of First Nations heritage and are simply living their lives, whether elderly, young, nurses, cooks, administrators, lawyers, doctors, teachers, politicians, surveyors, engineers, actors, artists, community leaders, biologists, hydro workers, farmers, entrepreneurs, fishermen, parents ... well, you get the idea. Those in this book are just a fraction of that group. In many ways most of them are ordinary individuals, yet, given the vast cultural and social gulf that still yawns between Aboriginal and non-Aboriginal communities and individuals in Canada, their stories, like all the others, are well worth knowing. Thanks for reading them.

1: You Are Who You Are

You can be whatever Indian you want to be. Whoever you are is what you are and you don't have to prove you're more native or less native—you are who you are. If you can accept that, that's perfectly good for everyone else too.

Lisa Webster-Gibson, b. 1966

Delaware Mohawk/Six Nations/Scottish Canadian from way back, Gabriola Island

Environmental assessment professional

Spoken-word and visual artist, rock 'n' roll drummer

Devoted mom

Individualist

Lisa Webster-Gibson, an environmental assessment expert in her professional life, dabbles on the side in what she describes as "a bit of odd art." She finds the act of creation therapeutic: taking the recognizable commonplace materials she uses and transforming them into something unanticipated by the observer.

First she looks for the whitened bones of small creatures that lie scattered on the forest floor or among the seaweed on the beach of her adopted home on Gabriola Island, just off Nanaimo on Vancouver Island. Then she sorts them, dyes them bright colours and reassembles them into something utterly different from their former incarnation as mice or fish or birds. A butterfly is created from a bird's skull, a flower from the bones of a mouse. "What I like about these pieces," Lisa observes, "are the reactions to them by people who don't know at first what they are made from."

Lisa Webster-Gibson
Courtesy the Committee for Native Employment Calendar

Initial delight at the beauty turns into revulsion when people realize what the pieces are made from, and then, finally, into acceptance. "There is so much stigma attached to bones. People automatically think of death and decay in relation to them," she says. But these are works of art that defy such characterization. Each individual bone is still in the form in which it naturally developed and later emerged from the decomposing body of some creature, but plays an unanticipated role as something beautiful rather than repulsive. Appreciating the pieces, Lisa says, "challenges people to move beyond their traditional prejudices, what they have been taught to think about bones as something gross or ugly, and look at them in another way. It makes them see something unexpected in an object they wouldn't necessarily want to look at if they had a choice."

Once they open their minds to the concept, she says, people tend to reach out to the pieces rather than recoil from them. That's what people need to do more with everything they encounter in life generally, she believes. "Look at whatever it is in front of you—a building, a blade of grass, anything—with awe and wonder. Look for what you don't expect to see, not what you have been taught to see or think you are going to see."

She is unconscious of the analogy as she speaks, but it's a philosophy that could easily be applied to the way that Canadian society tends to look at Aboriginal people. Lisa, who is Mohawk and Scottish Canadian, considers herself an individual with a distinct identity, with the potential (like everyone else) to startle and amaze if she is accepted for who she is when regarded with an open mind free of preconceived labels.

Too often, however, she is pigeonholed into the narrow box of whatever the observer's particular perception of native people happens to be. Sometimes that's hyperbolic—the feathered, moccasin-clad "noble, spiritual, wise" man or woman image—but more often it is harshly and unfairly negative. Rarely is it anything other than stereotyping, and at forty-seven years of age Lisa has run across almost every stereotype imaginable.

The irony is that none of the stereotypes apply either to her or to most of the people she knows who happen to be of Aboriginal heritage. The trick to dealing with this, she has learned, is to encourage people to start looking differently, to see what they don't expect to see—not a preconceived cliché of an Indian (whatever that means), but the individual who happens to be Lisa Webster-Gibson, who has Mohawk blood in her veins as well as Scottish Canadian ancestry—her bones, if you will, brightly coloured and assembled in a way that defies stereotyping in any manner.

Lisa's grandfather, Jim Moses, moved away from his Six Nations reserve in Ontario in 1923, when he was twelve years old. Like many other Canadians at the time, his parents had found that there wasn't enough work close to their own community. You had to move away for employment, or starve. Things hadn't improved much by the time Jim became an adult. In a radio interview that he gave several decades after leaving the reserve, Jim reminisced: "In those days, you couldn't buy a job." Jim had his technical certification as an electrician, but it didn't help. "I started working for the local farmers instead, alongside my dad."

In 1937 Jim married Lisa's grandmother, Ruby, who also hailed originally from the Six Nations reserve. It may well be that Lisa inherited her feisty attitude—and her robust belief in her own individuality—from her grandmother. Ruby, who was interviewed on the radio at the same time as Jim, talked about being raised by her parents on the reserve: "We were never taught anything about being Indians especially. We were just people, like everybody else. We were taught things at home, not because we were Indian but just because they were important things to know. We knew we were Indians. You never lose your culture. There is no way that you can lose it. That is you. It doesn't matter what anyone else thinks. You know who you are."

Ruby also recalled the cold reception that her young Indian family received from some of the local white families in Vineland, Ontario, where they settled down after getting married. "Jim isn't a fighter like I am," she said, "but I just felt we wanted respect, and

Lisa's Tóta, or great-grandfather, Patton.
Courtesy Lisa Webster-Gibson

they weren't going to wear me down. I used to tell the kids, 'Just hold your head up high, you're a person.'" Ruby stuck to her guns, and it worked. "Gradually they realized we were just people too and I forgot all about it, we all became good friends and would go to each other's houses and have parties and play cards together."

Perhaps it was a gentler place, if not time. More likely, Jim and Ruby were just lucky. The next two generations in the family had a vastly different experience. Their daughter Margaret, or Marg, met a Scottish Canadian named Daniel Webster in Guelph, Ontario, in the late 1950s. In 1966, their daughter Lisa was born in Wingham, Ontario.

A small town of about three thousand people near Lake Huron, Wingham is a long way from any Aboriginal community. "We were the only 'native' family in town," Lisa recalls. Prejudice was rife, despite the fact that her father was a well-respected schoolteacher. "There was prejudice, a lot of racism. When you're the only visible natives in a small town, you become a target."

There was also simply ignorance of who she was. "I would get asked questions like, 'Do you live in a tipi?' 'What's your Indian name?'" Lisa laughs now, but even the benign prejudice pursued her relentlessly into adulthood, along with the more negative constant questioning as to why native people didn't want to "better themselves" or "work harder" or "enjoy the benefits of being part of the mainstream," without any real interest in her answers.

"I got so fed up with people asking those kinds of questions without really wanting to understand who we are," Lisa says. "Even in my own home, in my own backyard, it would happen." She remembers calling her beloved cousin Jay for comfort one particularly bad day. They discussed their experiences of non-Aboriginal perceptions of native people, and the perplexity of encountering diehard negative beliefs that were based on ignorance and accompanied by little willingness to learn or change attitudes. Falling back on their shared sense of humour to deflect the pain inflicted by such entrenched discrimination, the two cousins cooked up an irreverent reference checklist for human resource managers wanting to hire a "genuine Indian."

"The idea harked back to when I was first hired by the Department of Indian and Northern Affairs, which is now Aboriginal Affairs and Northern Development Canada. That was in Vancouver, more than twenty years ago. I had my environmental studies qualifications by then. The human resource manager said to me proudly, 'You're a native woman in a technical field. There are only three of you in Canada doing this work. And we have two of you!' My jaw literally dropped. I couldn't believe someone would say something like that."

The concept that she had been hired because it permitted the manager to score points based on her "Indian-ness" was distasteful in the extreme to the young woman. "I felt like hiring me had nothing to do with me as a person, or my qualifications. It was completely objectionable to me as a First Nations person to be hired as a token that way. Who knew I was just a commodity?"

Hence the checklist for hiring your own genuine Indian: "Does he live on a reserve? Plus ten points! Does she drive a car with only one gear? Plus ten points! Does she have a graduate degree? Minus twenty points! Does she live in a nice condo in downtown Vancouver? Minus thirty points! We had about fifty of these items that you could use to score whether you were hiring a genuine Indian." Based on the stereotypes with which Lisa was all too familiar, the checklist provided a way to laugh away the hurt. More seriously, she reflects: "Everyone has such fixed ideas of what Indians, or First Nations, or Aboriginal people—whatever—should be, and those ideas have nothing to do whatsoever with who that individual actually is."

Lisa doesn't think of herself as being "half" Mohawk and "half" Scottish, for example. She finds it odd to try to characterize people of mixed heritage as being split up into two different things, or into fractions. Instead she sees herself as being an inseparable combination of two colours, or as wearing two skins at the same

Lisa Webster-Gibson
Courtesy Front Row Photography, Pat Sayer photo

time: "How can you be half something? Genetics is not divisive. It doesn't split someone into fractions. It combines two or more things together into a single whole being. In genetic terms, you simply can't be half of anything."

She also thinks of herself as just another person living in the world that is twenty-first-century British Columbia: getting the chores done around the airy, comfortable home she shares with her partner, Jack; doing her best to raise her son, Colin; pursuing her career; and helping First Nations communities with their environmental concerns. On her own time, she likes to perform. For several years she put her sense of humour to good use moonlighting as a successful stand-up comic at clubs and cafés throughout the

Lower Mainland of British Columbia. These days she is more into spoken-word performance, participating in "story slams" in Vancouver from time to time and hosting similar events on Gabriola Island. "It is really, really a lot of fun," she says fervently.

She also plays baseball for the "420s," her home team on Gabriola; she finished the Ironman competition in 2006, to challenge herself as so many people do when they turn forty (and she doubts she will do it again); she plays with the blue-eyed dog, Zebo, and teases her cats Steven and Bruce; and she whales away on weekends at her rock 'n' roll drum set. Since starting to drum a few years ago, she has been playing with a band that Jack and a few of his musical buddies co-founded. They practise regularly in the back shed; the band, unsurprisingly, is named Shed. It is enjoying modest success and in 2013 released its second CD.

Lisa is excited and inspired by the Idle No More protest movement that young Canadian Aboriginal activists started in late 2012 and the opportunity it has provided for all Canadians to better understand the hopes and dreams of Aboriginal people. The movement has drawn many non-Aboriginal individuals and groups sympathetic to the cause of human rights. "I feel very deeply affected by Idle No More and what it represents as a protest against the way in which our existence is being compromised and degraded by the actions of governments. That's something we all share in common, no matter who we are. I hope it means Canadians start seeing us in a different way because of this, put aside old prejudices and empathize with us instead."

It would be infinitely better for everyone, she believes, if people could start looking at Aboriginal people like her, doing the things they love to do, simply as individuals who happen to be of First Nations heritage—to whatever extent, greater or lesser—and just appreciate them for who and what they are, whatever colours they may be comprised of and in whatever shape their bones are assembled.

That includes acknowledging their cultural history and accepting both the negative and the positive aspects of it. It also means using that knowledge and acceptance to interact positively with people of Aboriginal heritage as products of their history and culture, instead of holding their origins against them: "I've never had any issue with being combined Mohawk Delaware and Scottish Canadian," she says. "So why should anyone else?"

Colin, born in 1997, has been a major influence on how she looks at the world. "He's a really cool kid. He knows exactly who he is. He doesn't let it limit him or his sense of identity. He accepts everyone for who they are and doesn't divide them along the lines of culture and colour. He knows he's different," she adds. "He has Mohawk blood in him, with totally brown skin and black hair. But he also doesn't make anything of it. It's just the way it is."

Colin has hyperlexia, a precocious ability to read—which he does voraciously—partnered with a contradictory and frustrating inability to find the right words to express himself in his own terms. "He has complex thoughts, but he has a hard time finding ways to express them. He usually falls back on learned phrases, like similes or analogies, to get his point across," says Lisa.

When Colin speaks, you have to listen carefully to understand what he's saying. It's another lesson in crossing boundaries that has a broader application for Lisa: "I think the biggest communication barrier between people generally is not listening properly. I'm a talker, not a listener by nature, but I have had a decade of communicating with a child with language issues. You develop a listening ability that you take everywhere with you. I treat everyone now as if they had hyperlexia! I listen really hard. I get along way better with people as a result of that attitude."

Lisa hopes for a future for Colin in which he is both free of the constraints of stereotyping and retains the strong sense of identity and individuality he has inherited from his confident mother. "We all want that really, don't we?" she asks. "Whoever we may be, wherever we are from."

That sense of individuality and pride in identity is a legacy for which she in turn remains profoundly grateful to Colin's grandfather Daniel, who passed away in early 2013. Intensely proud of his

Scottish heritage, Daniel taught his children to be proud of it as well: Lisa can recite her Scottish lineage as easily as her Mohawk ancestry. Daniel is also the one who instilled in them knowledge of and pride in being Mohawk. "He was a history buff and he taught us about the Six Nations, he took us to powwows and helped us learn Indian crafts when we were small," she recalls.

Her mother, Margaret, wasn't as fortunate. "Growing up in a white community in the 1940s, my mother had a very confused sense of her cultural identity." Lisa recalls making a remark once about a woman with strong traditional practices; her mother became defensive, saying that she had not been raised to be traditional. "I said to her, 'Mom, you can be whatever Indian you want to be,'" says Lisa. "Whoever you are is what you are and you don't have to prove you're more native or less native—you are who you are."

Her mother was already in her sixties by then. "I think it was the first time anyone had ever told her it was okay to define herself whatever way she wanted. I'm so glad I didn't grow up in that world she did—when native people couldn't vote because of their ethnicity and the women were forced to give up their Aboriginal identity if they married the wrong-coloured man." (Before the 1985 passage of Bill C-31, which amended the *Indian Act* to remove discriminatory provisions and restore equality of rights, an Aboriginal woman who married a non-Aboriginal man automatically lost her Indian status under the act, as did her children.)

All the same, like her mother and many of her contemporaries, Lisa does find herself sometimes juggling two distinct non-Aboriginal and Aboriginal worlds, particularly in her professional life. "After twenty-one years working in the federal government, it is hard to believe but the bureaucratic system still wants me to choose which side I am on. Why should I have to pick a side?" Unlike her mother, however, Lisa has greater freedom to stand up to those who suggest native people should choose between their two realities. She says emphatically: "I am *not* going to sacrifice the values of one world for the other." Indeed, Lisa thinks that some-

Lisa's parents, Daniel Webster and Margaret Moses, on their wedding day.
Courtesy Lisa Webster-Gibson

one trying to put her in a box in that fashion is guilty of questioning her identity. "I think they have a problem. It's certainly not my problem—I know exactly who I am and I'm very comfortable with it."

It may not be too late for her mother to put aside the prejudice and hard lessons of her childhood and become comfortable with her Mohawk identity in this modern world. It has certainly not been too late for Lisa and, with any luck, working out his identity will never be a struggle that her son has to grapple with.

"You are who you are," she repeats softly, looking over at Colin, frowning in fierce concentration as he plays computer games at the kitchen table, his dark curly hair glinting in the warm August afternoon sunshine. "If you can accept that, that's perfectly good for everyone else too."

2: One Hundred Percent Me

I'm unafraid to try anything. That's important, because to bring the story or image across—it takes a lot of self-exploration to capture the emotion, to create the piece of art. That comes back to me putting into it not just what I have learned or my experiences but who I am as a person.

John Marston (Qap'u'luq), b. 1978
Chemainus First Nation, Ladysmith
Artist
Storyteller
Navigator through cultural boundaries
Husband to Ashley; dad to Noah, Tate and Sophie

"I see my artwork as a unique opportunity for telling stories that goes beyond simply creating beautiful objects of art," says John Marston. "I put 100 percent of me into every piece. If someone really looks at that piece, really connects to the emotions and experiences in it, then they are seeing me in it, not just as an artist but as what kind of person I am, and who I am."

This is who John Marston is: an artist to the core. The stories he has to tell pour ceaselessly out of him, passing through his innately

John Marston (Qap'u'luq)
Courtesy John and Ashley Marston

gifted and immensely skilled hands into colourful and exquisitely crafted painted wood carvings. It is almost impossible for him to think of doing anything else. "Every piece is a part of me, part of who I am," John says quietly. "My heart and soul goes into each one of them."

Because of his intense investment in the art pieces he creates, John often finds it enormously difficult to say goodbye to them. In 2010, to mark that year's Olympic Winter Games, the Vancouver Airport Authority commissioned John to create a massive work comprising nine giant carved paddles, to be installed in the domestic terminal at Vancouver Airport. "A great deal of my teachings about art, my spirituality, what I have learned about culture and life—all that is living in that work," John explains. "It was almost like a grieving process to leave it behind after all the time I spent working on it. After something like that, I really have to step back and refocus all my energy into what I will do next."

That's a familiar sensation to most professional artists: the reality that each work is integrally connected to identity and experience, and letting it go is akin to saying goodbye to part of oneself. It is also a sensation John has had to become accustomed to over a remarkable and prolific career to date for such a young artist. His work is carried by high-end galleries and museums in Victoria, Vancouver, Seattle and New York, and coveted by art aficionados worldwide. A carved canoe graces the lobby of a Swiss bank. *White Light*, a carving that expresses a prayer for safe travels, is installed in Nanaimo Airport on Vancouver Island.

In September 2009, John received his first British Columbia Creative Achievement Award for Aboriginal art. Only thirty-one years old at the time, he was one of the youngest recipients of the award that year. That wasn't surprising to those who know him. John was born among Coast Salish artists. Many of the stories he tells through his art are ones he grew up with; carving is in his blood and he has been doing it since he was just eight years old. "I remember my mother giving me a knife and telling me to go carve with my dad," John recalls. "I had never been

John Marston with White Light, installation at the Nanaimo Airport.
Courtesy John and Ashley Marston

John speaking at the unveiling of White Light at the Nanaimo Airport in September
2011. *Courtesy John and Ashley Marston*

allowed to do that before. I ran straight downstairs to my dad's workshop with the knife in my hand and told him, 'Mom said I can carve now!'"

John's English–Ojibway father, David, was delighted at his young son's enthusiasm and enjoyed his company in the workshop as the boy played at making his first piece, a miniature logging truck. For David, carving was a way to relax in spare time, and throughout John's childhood father and son spent many happy hours together working on their respective projects. John's mother, Jane, from Chemainus First Nation on Vancouver Island, is also an accomplished carver. The two have collaborated on several projects, the most recent of which is a welcome figure erected at the doors of the Tillicum Lelum Aboriginal Friendship Centre in Nanaimo.

"When I was much younger, my mom also worked a lot with the great artist Simon Charlie, who lived in Duncan," John says. Simon Charlie's cedar totem poles grace the Parliament Buildings in Ottawa, the Royal British Columbia Museum in Victoria and numerous other official institutions both in Canada and abroad, and in 2001 the highly respected Aboriginal artist and elder was recognized with the Order of British Columbia for his achievements and his contributions to the province. "Simon and Mom worked together on many totem poles and art pieces over the years. He was a constant presence and a great mentor to me from a very young age," John says.

Between Charlie and his talented parents, the aspiring young carver could not have dreamed of better mentors or a more supportive environment in which to foster his artistic skills. "Looking back, I know I was very lucky to grow up like that," John reflects. "I didn't appreciate that then—I just thought that was the way life was, carving on weekends and after school with these adults who liked to carve too." John clearly recalls the first "real" carving he did under his mother and Charlie's supervision, a salmon plaque completed when he was nine years old. "One of the things they taught me is that when you are still learning like that, you must

John with the Welcome Figure, carved with his mother, Jane Marston, and installed at the Tillicum Lelum Aboriginal Friendship Centre in June 2011.
Courtesy John and Ashley Marston

give away everything you make. So I gave that piece to my mom. She still has it."

John's carving training was in the traditional First Nations style, learned at his parents' sides as well as from great artists like Simon Charlie, Silas Coon, Shawn Karpes, Wayne Young and John's older brother, Luke Marston. "I was very fortunate. Simon taught me the stories told through our art and he showed me how to carve. That influence is still present in my work." He was also lucky enough to have an excellent art teacher at high school, Anne-Marie Cobalt, who taught him the basics of conventional art skills. "She also taught me a lot about being a professional artist. She was wonderful."

After graduating, however, John didn't go to art school. "I went straight from high school to working for a living as an artist," he says. "I had everyone around me to teach me what I needed to know, and I had no limits placed on me. If I wanted to try carving something, Mom would say, 'Go ahead then and carve it.'" That unqualified support for whatever he wanted to try was a huge influence on how he approached his work as an adult and full-time professional artist.

"It's still a major influence. I'm unafraid to try anything. That's important, because to bring the story or image across—it takes a lot of self-exploration to capture the emotion, to create the piece of art. That comes back to me putting into it not just what I have learned or my experiences but who I am as a person. What I put into each piece," he repeats firmly, "is 100 percent me."

He makes it sound easy. The reality of getting to where he is now—successfully making a living from his art, represented in major galleries and winning artistic awards—was a lot tougher. After he left school, even though he had been wielding a carving knife for years, John was still just starting out on his artistic journey, and he knew he had a lot of work to do. From Simon Charlie and other elders he began learning the legends of his people and the stories of the places in which he and his ancestors lived, all commonly portrayed in Coast Salish art.

He was also taught the correct traditional art forms and the proper processes to produce conventional First Nations shapes and figures. "You have to learn all those things before you can express your own ideas as an artist," John says. "That's true of every art form, and it's a good teaching. You learn the steps, and at the beginning you follow them in everything you do."

But after a few years, John reached a point where the traditional art forms started to become obstacles rather than opportunities for creation. "I had worked so much on recreating old, archival pieces that I finally hit a wall. I didn't know where to go from there. I felt like I was just making pieces that were ours in a time-honoured sense, but which weren't mine in any artistic sense."

John had to somehow achieve a difficult balancing act: continuing to apply what he had learned from master carvers in telling his ancestors' stories, and honouring them through his artwork in his own unique way. "I finally realized that those traditional forms had become barriers to my development. To grow as an artist and as a person I had to find a way to set aside the barriers, and to a certain extent the traditional teachings, and start creating pieces that still honoured the stories but which *weren't* done the way I had always been shown."

That was harder than he had anticipated. He was still only twenty-four years old at the time. Until then, his artwork had always felt like a safe place. It was integrally tied into his culture, with every aspect of the work undertaken through well-known and long-established processes. Taking the leap into the unknown realm of self-expression, unencumbered by conventional rules and cultural themes, was extraordinarily difficult. "I felt completely lost at first," John recalls. "I was searching for spiritual inspiration. I kept going back and forth between the original work, which was safe, and looking for a new, unrealized direction. It was a very confusing time."

During the chaos of that transformative period, Simon Charlie tried to help the young artist with advice and feedback, discussing the traditional stories with John and explaining their nuances and richness in an effort to inspire him. Then, suddenly

John working on his canoe, with son Noah supervising closely.
Courtesy John and Ashley Marston

and unexpectedly, Simon died. "He was such an important person to me and such a significant influence on my life as well as my work that I felt utterly lost all over again," says John, remembering the pain of that time vividly. "It was very traumatic."

It was also, however, the trigger point for John's breakthrough. "At first I really wondered what I was going to do. Then I realized I had to make a choice. That was the moment when I stopped looking for the correct way of doing things and started just working from the heart." It took a lot of courage. "I had to really believe in myself. But it was definitely the right thing to do. My work became cleaner and more defined, and more of it started consistently getting picked up by galleries." He has continued to make his living by his carvings ever since.

One of the galleries that spotted John's talent early was the Alcheringa Gallery in Victoria. Specializing in indigenous art forms, curator Elaine Monds has been an avid supporter of John's work. When she invited him to participate in a cultural art exchange in Papua, New Guinea, she also became responsible for another significant and transformative life experience for John.

"Elaine asked me to go to New Guinea in 2006, and spend a few weeks with Sepik carver Teddy Balangu in Palembei Village," John says. "She had travelled to the Palembei and other villages several times already, and she thought it would be a great thing for me to accompany her on her next trip and experience a completely different indigenous environment." Documentary filmmakers Peter Campbell and Art Holbrook would record the journey, as well as Teddy's subsequent trip to Vancouver to undertake a carving commission at the Museum of Anthropology.

John was simultaneously thrilled and terrified at the opportunity. "I decided to go, but I had heard all these horror stories about man-eating crocodiles and even that if the crocodiles didn't get you, the people would," he says, laughing now at the recollection. "At the time, I was pretty intimidated." Elaine, smiling knowingly, simply told the young carver to expect the unexpected.

The heat, colours, smells, strange food and exotic wildlife were all among the catalogue of overwhelming foreign experiences for the young traveller. What was truly a surprise to him, however, was an enormous shifting of the ground beneath his feet—both literally and figuratively.

He had never been outside Coast Salish territory before. Thousands of kilometres from home, tucked into a dugout being paddled down a narrow jungle stream flanked by exotic jungle flora, he found himself utterly out of context and flailing about for a way to conduct himself as a First Nations person in unfamiliar territory. "In the beginning, I felt I had no connection to that land or those waters," he says. "There was nothing of my heritage there to draw upon at first. I knew what I was supposed to do in my own territory but I had never turned my mind before to having to do it somewhere else, in a foreign place."

John knew some of the protocols associated with being a First Nations traveller—thank the hosts for allowing you to speak and to share their territory, for example—but came home understanding for the first time that he had a great deal more to learn about his own culture. "I had spent all this time learning about art, and the stories told through our traditional art forms, but I hadn't learned much about *being* Coast Salish, and about our songs and our practices. That's something I came home determined to do and have been doing ever since."

John's trip to Papua New Guinea—subsequently showcased in the documentary *Killer Whale and Crocodile,* directed by Peter Campbell—was an enormously significant event for him personally as well as professionally. "I learned so many things from that trip, about people and about life." For a start, he quickly realized that none of the horror stories he had heard about Papua New Guinea were true. After he had been warmly greeted and cared for everywhere he went, the light bulb went on that he had been as guilty of harbouring the kind of uninformed prejudices about the native Papuans that non-First Nations people often harbour about Aboriginal people. "But of course, you can't know that until you get there and actually meet the people and get to know them."

John also came home with a reinvigorated commitment to his contemporary approach to producing artwork. That doesn't mean sacrificing his traditional teachings: traditional First Nations art pieces, John explains, tell the quintessential stories of what the ancestors did and how they lived. "We have to honour those teachings and stories. They're vital to our identity and understanding our history. But we also need to tell the stories of what we are doing today, which is what I'm doing. So much has changed, and so many more changes keep happening. We are constantly learning." That's why today's stories will be fundamental for people to know and understand one hundred years from now, John says. "This is a visual way of recording those changes, our experiences, and what we're learning."

In a sense, he's finally doing what his ancestors always did, in his own unique way. His unconventional form also allows him to cross cultural boundaries. "For example, after I came back from New Guinea the pieces I worked on tell the story of my experiences there, and relate them to the impact on me here, both personally and as an artist." Day's end in the tropics is evoked in glowing gold and red in *Palembei Sunset*; a giant two-layered panel pays *Homage to the Sepik*—'ehhue'p syuth—incorporating both First Nations and native New Guinean symbols. "It simply wouldn't be possible to tell those stories using only traditional methods," he explains.

John hopes to undertake more cultural art exchange projects. He also plans to pay a return visit to Papua New Guinea one day with his son Noah, who has a namesake in Teddy's grandson. "While we were in Palembei, Teddy asked us if we would offer a name for his grandson, which is a great honour," John explains. "Namesakes are highly respected there, so I suggested the name Noah, after my son. Teddy thought it was most appropriate, too, since they had been experiencing the highest flood levels in twenty-five years at the time!"

He also dreams of harvesting a tree in British Columbia using traditional methods and taking it to Japan, which he visited in 2008, to carve it there. "I want to do it the proper way right from the start, walking through the forest and finding the right tree according to traditional teachings, then finding a way to take it to Japan with me. The organization I've worked with in Japan wants to do it, and has even said where it should be done—on a mountaintop, by a shrine. How amazing would that be?"

It hasn't happened yet, but John feels certain it will. In the meantime, he is working on a canoe, combining his traditional knowledge with his innate artistic skill to create a vessel that will honour the ways of the ancestors in a contemporary and compelling visual design. He would also like to teach. "I'd like to share what I've learned in the same way I was taught. I am sure I'll learn from that too."

John is also already planning the body of work for his next show at a Vancouver gallery. He is lost in a reverie of ideas, exploration, experiences and teachings, visualizing the work that lies ahead, as he invests himself yet again into the art: heart and soul, professional and personal, unafraid and—as always—100 percent John Marston, artist to the core.

3: Travels Across the Medicine Line

I will always keep fighting to see both indigenous and Western principles and approaches considered to be of equal value in caring for people, and to expand understanding of what it means for Aboriginal people—for all of us—to be healthy and whole.

Lyana Patrick, b. 1974
Stellat'en First Nation (Carrier), Acadian/Scottish
Nadleh Bun (Fraser Lake)/Vancouver
Vanier Scholar
MA, indigenous governance
PhD student in community and regional planning, UBC
Filmmaker

W hen I browsed through Lyana Patrick's résumé, I thought that it would be simpler to summarize what she *hasn't* accomplished in the two decades of her adult life: in short, not much.

In 2004, after completing a master's degree in indigenous governance at the University of Victoria, she qualified for a Fulbright Scholarship to study at the University of Washington, in its Native Voices Program. For her project, she chose to produce a documentary film called *Travels Across the Medicine Line* that would examine how Aboriginal people would be affected by heightened security measures at the US–Canadian border in a post-9/11 world.

The 1794 *Treaty of London* between the British and American governments, or the *Jay Treaty* as it is better known, confirmed the rights of indigenous peoples on both sides of the border to move freely across it as they had for thousands of years, following ancient north-to-south spiritual, familial and trading routes. But with the occurrence of the events of 9/11, freedom of movement across the border was severely curtailed. First Nations people suddenly found themselves entangled in an artificial barrier not of their own making that prevented them from carrying on many of the traditional activities to which they were accustomed.

For the young filmmaker, the story she wanted to tell went beyond truculent border guards and frustrated travellers. The border became an apt metaphor for the disconnection between the cultural and traditional lives of Aboriginal people in Canada on the one hand and the artificial structure and restrictions that the *Indian Act* forced on them through the process of colonization.

Modern Western life and the structural frameworks in which Canadians operate—whether regulatory, spiritual, socio-economic or otherwise—were leaving little room, if any, for ancient traditions and values to be acknowledged or respected. That had had disastrous results for the indigenous peoples of both Canada and the United States. It was a theme that Lyana had contemplated a great deal already, even at her young age, and it was beginning to

Lyana Patrick
Cherryl Williams photo

take on increasing importance in how she viewed the world and her role in it.

By the time she completed the film in 2005, she was mulling over what that might mean in terms of her own future. She had already garnered herself a degree in creative writing and history from the University of Victoria. She had also interned as a scriptwriter on the popular homegrown television series *North of 60*, and spent time in New Zealand working as a production assistant with Maori documentary filmmakers, exploring the cultural significance of *moko*, or traditional tattoos. Along the way, she had chalked up several awards and scholarships, including a National Aboriginal Achievement Foundation scholarship and a Canadian Native Arts Fund grant.

But filmmaking, while a passionate interest of hers, wasn't enough to satisfy her increasing hunger to work to improve the lives of indigenous people. Putting the filmmaking aside, at least for the time being, Lyana enrolled at the University of British Columbia to get her medical school prerequisites under way.

While at UBC she seized the opportunity to work in the Division of Aboriginal Peoples' Health. Director Dr. Evan Adams,[2] who hails from the Sliammon First Nation in Powell River, was deputy provincial health officer with responsibility for Aboriginal health in British Columbia. He was also a film and television actor, perhaps best known for his role as Thomas Builds-the-Fire in the 1999 movie *Smoke Signals.* Lyana felt right at home immediately. "Evan was a huge inspiration to me," she says. "His career involved both interests of mine. He was—and still is—incredibly busy, but I felt if he could do it, so could I. I feel very lucky to have had the chance to work with him and get to know him."

Although working with Adams was inspirational, her study program was another matter. Lyana had her sights set on working in Aboriginal communities one day in the field of mental health and addictions. She had no doubt in her mind she could achieve

2 "Working Really Hard Just to Get to a Normal Place", page 207

her goal. With a track record of high academic achievement, sound critical analysis and years of sheer hard work already behind her, there was nothing to suggest she would not succeed. All the same, school proved more testing than she could have imagined.

"It was stressful for everyone, but especially for the indigenous students. There's a perception out there that we get special treatment, or have it somehow easier with lower standards being set for us. But I felt the opposite was true. The expectations of the teachers were much higher for us than for our non-Aboriginal colleagues. We had to do twice as much work to prove ourselves."

That was in large part because of an academic resistance toward approaching health care from an Aboriginal perspective, something Lyana had not anticipated. To her, incorporating indigenous medicine into treatment practices was simply common sense. To her teachers, that was heresy.

"Western medicine treats the body, not the person. It's very set in its ways. But if you are really going to apply critical thinking to health care, then you can't separate cultural and emotional perspectives out from the physical analysis. When it comes to Aboriginal health care, you have to understand what Aboriginal people have experienced through the history of colonization—the loss of language and spiritual strength, the abuses of the residential-school system and all the rest—and you have to know something about indigenous beliefs and medicine and cultural practices. You have to be competent at culturally appropriate treatment practices as well as traditional Western medicine or you can't possibly treat the whole person effectively."

Rather than embracing this holistic approach to medicine, her non-Aboriginal teachers challenged her. "I was constantly faced with an incredibly dismissive attitude when I tried to include Aboriginal experiences and stories into the work. I would get challenged over and over again. Everything has to be evidence-based and quantitative. Is it science? Can you prove it? But how do you quantify experience, or cultural practices, or the destructive impact of colonization?"

The prerequisites she needed to qualify for medical school included biology courses. The same resistance to alternative concepts or analysis was embedded in her natural science classes. "If I challenged their science—like the theory that indigenous people came to North America over the Bering Strait Bridge—I would be dismissed out of hand, even though that theory is still unproven. But if I tried to introduce an alternative viewpoint, such as our origin stories, that would be treated as myth rather than scientific theory. I would be told to prove it, or leave it out. There was simply no acceptance of Aboriginal scientific theory or analysis."

Lyana stuck to her guns, pulling out all the stops to ensure she knew the traditional science inside out as well as the indigenous themes she was attempting to include in her work. She maintains a positive attitude toward that experience. "Having to do all that additional analysis and critical thinking certainly has made me sharper, much more aware of the issues and very capable of defending my beliefs and cultural approach," she says. "I don't regret that part at all."

Lyana also believes that the kind of approach she was taking helped to raise awareness among the faculty and other students, a development she thinks is essential. "The reality is that every doctor in Canada is going to treat an indigenous person at some point. We have to try and shift people's mindsets so that they will believe they'll do a better job as doctors if they take this kind of approach. We need to encourage them to take the lead in embracing the approach and incorporating an understanding of Aboriginal culture and history into the way they practise medicine.

"That will put them in a much better, more respectful relationship with their patients and ultimately give them a much better chance of success in treatment. It will also have a huge impact on the health care system if the disproportionately negative statistics around Aboriginal health start improving as a result. It's hard to see why anyone wouldn't support that. That kind of outcome helps everyone in the system, regardless of who it is—doctors, patients, people on the waiting lists, the taxpayer, you name it."

For Lyana, however, change did not come soon enough. While some students and teachers were open to her ideas, the intractable weight of a centuries-old medical system stuck in a deeply entrenched rut eventually became overwhelming. By 2010, she had become completely disheartened. "I started to feel that if I did want to stay in medicine, the only way to succeed was to put aside my cultural values. I simply couldn't do that." On the cusp of being accepted into medical school, Lyana made the difficult decision that a career in orthodox medicine was not for her.

A few months earlier, she had learned she was pregnant. Wanting to spend time with her husband and child played a role in her decision, but ultimately she simply wasn't happy with the direction that she was going in professionally. "I know that for some people medicine is a lifelong dream and it's the most meaningful thing they can think of doing. I had put five years of incredibly hard work into it based on that kind of dream. But it wasn't the right choice for me. I still wanted to work in the mental health field, I still wanted to work with addictions, but I wanted to do that in a different way."

Lyana had personal reasons for wanting to work in this area. She was an adult when she first started hearing about the residential-school experiences of her father, Archie, and she had only heard the full story for the first time in 2008 when Archie took a physical abuse claim to the government under the *Indian Residential Schools Settlement Agreement*. The 2007 agreement set up a claims and compensation process for survivors of the residential-school system, and created the Truth and Reconciliation Commission to promote public awareness of the history and impacts of the residential schools in Canada. "It was so moving to hear him speak about his experience," Lyana says. "It was visceral. It was the first time I really understood the intergenerational impact on so many families of the residential-school system.

"I was so lucky in comparison to my father. I grew up with a lot of love and encouragement at home. My father worked incredibly hard and became a teacher, politician and administrator, despite

Lyana with her husband, Jim, and son, Kazimir, in 2011.
Courtesy Solomon Rosenberg

his terrible experiences. He is a fluent speaker of the Carrier language and he helped establish the Yinka Déné Language Institute in 1988. He still works hard on language issues. My mother, Sandra, who is French Acadian, has a very strong sense of social justice and she instilled that in me. Everything I am doing now honours what my parents have worked for all their lives as well."

As Lyana pondered her options in 2010, at a loss as to what to do next, she contemplated starting a doctorate degree. "I still wanted to be engaged in meaningful, invigorating work. I knew I wanted to find new, culturally competent ways to approach Aboriginal mental health and addictions, and I was hoping to build my documentary film background into that somehow, as a tool for sharing human experiences and for educating." Her only problem was finding the best way to achieve those goals.

She then had a serendipitous encounter with Leonie Sandercock, a UBC School of Community and Regional Planning (SCARP) professor. Sandercock listened carefully to what Lyana had been thinking about, and suggested she enrol at SCARP. "I knew nothing about planning! But when I realized community planning is a very effective way to influence health care, I also figured out this was an amazing opportunity to address all the things I had been talking about."

Lyana promptly applied to SCARP's PhD program and was accepted in September 2011. Barely six months later she was awarded a Vanier Scholarship, one of Canada's most prestigious and rigorously vetted academic grants. The scholarship will fully fund the completion of her doctorate in cultural safety in addictions and mental health planning with urban indigenous populations. Two years into the course, there were no regrets over leaving medical school behind. "I am so happy and excited to be doing this work," she says. "It's going to take me exactly where I want to go."

Lyana is now researching addictions and mental health from a planning rather than a medical angle, and is again working toward bringing cultural and traditional values into the process as a way to address the needs of First Nations communities from an indigenous perspective. "The time is ripe for a change from the very restrictive planning paradigm created for First Nations communities by the *Indian Act,* with its reserve boundaries and colonial restrictions that are still embedded in it, to reclaim a vision of communities that are structured around a more comprehensive approach that factors in everything that impacts on health and involves everyone," Lyana says.

"What I like about a planning approach is it ties everything together. It doesn't treat different aspects of the community in isolation. It's like treating a person with a specific disease. It's better to take a holistic look at everything about that person, what they do, what they eat, how they think, what influences their behaviour, not just the part of the body that is affected."

When we look at the health care needs of a community, Lyana

says, everything about that community needs to be examined, not just its physical infrastructure. That's important, of course, because it's good to know, for example, whether members of the community have adequate transportation to get to a doctor when needed. But as Lyana points out, unless the community's collective history and trauma are also considered in the planning equation, all of the infrastructure in the world won't make any difference.

"You can build new schools and create all kinds of economic opportunities but if you don't address the emotional and spiritual needs of the community in the planning process, you're simply recreating the problem. If you don't deal with addictions and related health issues, you'll still get high dropout rates from school and people spending all the money they're making in their new jobs on drugs or alcohol."

What Lyana is researching is a concept called therapeutic planning. "You look at housing, transportation, education infrastructure and economic development—all these elements of community planning—as a whole." Rather than simply using statistics to drive planning formulas, such as saying that if you have this number of people and this amount of land, you need this number of houses or schools, therapeutic planning is based on what is required to make a community healthy and whole. "It's quite a different approach that emphasizes the importance of stories and storytelling in the planning process."

Lyana wants to look at what is working well, not just at what may need fixing. "There's no shortage of research out there telling us what's wrong with the health care system and that it's repeatedly failed indigenous people. I'm interested in the possibilities for doing something right. Where are our success stories? There are people and communities out there doing really good work, and I want to explore how they're doing it and what we can do to replicate that success. How can we envision change on a big scale, while involving people at the local level in creating change tailored to their needs and circumstances? It might seem naive or idealistic to talk about creating change on a big scale, but I also believe in dreaming big and if I land somewhere a little closer to earth, then that's okay too!"

Lyana plans to apply what she has learned to the urban Vancouver community with which she is most familiar, having lived in the city for so many years. "It will be challenging, but it's so important given the huge indigenous population we have here." She also dreams one day of working in her ancestral Carrier territory. "That's not easy with a non-Aboriginal husband whose work is here, but it's vital for both of us to make sure my son, Kazimir, is able to learn about his heritage and his culture, so we are going to make sure we find a way to do that somehow."

Kazimir, also known as Kaz, was born in 2010 and is "a little force of nature!" He also motivates Lyana to nurture "a cultural internal landscape of the mind" as she lives and works in urban twenty-first-century Vancouver. "It's so important to hold onto our indigenous culture in our daily lives, and it's hard to do that here. I've sometimes found myself wondering what is indigenous about me anymore when I live here in the city, drive to work at UBC, and live in this suburban house in a big city. How does Kazimir learn who he is and where he comes from?"

For Lyana, it comes back to how she lives her life and what she teaches her son. "It's drawing on those ancient indigenous values and principles about cherishing community and family, working hard, taking responsibility and treating everyone with respect. Those things make me strong in the times I am away from my ancestral lands."

Those are the same values, of course, that she brought to her medical studies and is now applying in her planning research. "What I am bringing to the work I do is the knowledge of those ancient values and the stories. It is old knowledge and an old approach from an indigenous perspective, but still a relatively new concept in modern planning and medicine."

Lyana finds that it's still a struggle sometimes to have that knowledge recognized on its own merits and given the same kind of respect as orthodox methodologies. She was therefore

Lyana's young son, Kazimir, is teaching her the importance of connection to culture—as well as patience.
Courtesy Lyana Patrick

thrilled in the summer of 2012 when the Faculty of Medicine at UBC approached her to help put together a compulsory ten-hour course for first year medical students called Doctor, Patient and Society. "It was the first time that an indigenous course was a compulsory part of the curriculum for every student. I couldn't say no!" Ancient traditional techniques may finally be finding their way across the medicine line into orthodox approaches, one tiny step at a time, she says. "I think it will make a huge difference eventually."

Ultimately, Lyana says, there is no reason why the indigenous world and the Western world cannot be bridged to everyone's benefit, whether it is in medicine, planning or indeed any aspect of community health and well-being.

"That's what I want to keep working toward. I may have left medicine behind but in whatever field I am working, I will always keep fighting to see both sets of principles or values considered to be of equal value in caring for people, and to expand understanding of what it means for Aboriginal people—for all of us—to be healthy and whole."

Thoughts from Puuglas (Jody Wilson-Raybould)

b. 1971

Cape Mudge (We Wai Kai), Quadra Island (Kwakwaka'wakw)

BC Regional Chief, Assembly of First Nations

(interviewed in 2007)

As a twelve-year-old in 1983, I watched my father, Bill, an Aboriginal rights activist, on television in Ottawa. He was talking to then prime minister Pierre Trudeau about the recognition of Aboriginal rights in the Constitution.

My dad said to Trudeau that he had two daughters at home watching, and that one of them would be prime minister one day. That philosophy that anything is possible remains at the forefront of everything I aspire to. I want all Aboriginal people to have the ability to be who they want to be, and not have any person or institution dictate who and what we should be. I want my nieces to be the prime minister or national chief, or whatever they choose.

We have endured a lot. Where the connection to cultural identity has been lost, many Aboriginal people live with a constant sense of contradiction and compromise. The challenge is trying to live in two worlds, while currently being ill-equipped to live in either one. But when we are culturally strong in our own world, Aboriginal people are strong living in any world. The key is being able to control one's life. It's about being able to make decisions over how that life unfolds.

Katherine Palmer Gordon photo

4: First-Class Citizen

I tell the kids, just live with a good heart and a good mind, and just do the best that you can every day. When you live your life that way, even if you lose your discipline a little bit and stray from the Red Path a little, you will always come back. You will learn. You'll have a good life.

Wayne Gino Odjick, b. 1970

Iroquois/Algonquin

Kitigan Zibi Anishinabeg First Nation, Maniwaki, Quebec/ Musqueam, Vancouver

Former Canucks National Hockey League player

Successful businessman

Youth mentor

Avid golfer and reader

Don't *ever* not return a book you borrow from Gino Odjick. Apart from being "about the worst thing" you could do to this man, who cherishes every book he owns and whose idea of a great evening is settling back on the couch with a paperback, you really don't want to get on the wrong side of a six-foot-three, ninety-eight-kilogram former professional National Hockey League player whose nickname was once "the Algonquin Assassin."

"I had a teacher in Grade 1 who introduced me to reading," Gino explains, "and I've had a love affair with books ever since. When I was playing hockey, I would read about 150 books a year while I was on the road. I still read a lot, mostly self-improvement books but history too, biography—anything, really, so long as it's good." Reading, he adds, has helped him get through some tough times. "A good book allows you to just disappear inside it and forget everything else that's going on around you. I love that about my books."

Gino's well-honed literary streak is probably something most hockey fans don't know about the former Canucks player, who remains more famous for his record for all-time penalty minutes in a Vancouver jersey over the course of his twelve-year career in the NHL. Look Gino up on the internet and you'll find him featured in dozens of videos of on-ice brawls. The media started dubbing him "the Enforcer," and his fans adored Gino's heavyweight style on the ice and his passion and sheer strength as he dropped the gloves time and again to fight for his team on the rink.

But Gino was always as thoughtful about his battles on the ice as he was (and still is) about his reading choices. It was simply about looking after his teammates. "I had a job to do," he explains. "I didn't fight for the sake of fighting or to prove how tough I was. My role was to create space for my teammates to play with peace of mind, knowing I was watching their backs. That let them focus on what they needed to do to win the game. Hockey was always about winning, not fighting."

Being a team player was a role that came naturally to Gino, who had strong childhood roots in the tiny Maniwaki community of Kitigan Zibi Anishinabeg First Nation in Quebec, two hours north of

Gino Odjick
Courtesy Vancouver Canucks

Ottawa. Gino was the middle child of seven, and the only boy. Holding his own against six sisters was no mean feat, even for a big, strong kid like Gino. From his sisters and his mother, the young boy also learned a healthy respect for the wisdom and strength of women that he has carried with him throughout his adult life.

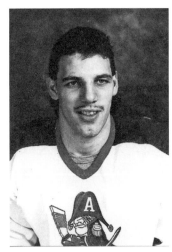

Top: Gino was brought up in a large, loving family, and has carried on the tradition with eight children of his own. *Courtesy Odjick family*

Above left: Gino's work with Peter Leech in youth mentoring workshops takes him to communities all over British Columbia. *Courtesy Peter Leech*

Above right: Early in his professional hockey career, Gino played for the Milwaukee Admirals. *Courtesy Milwaukee Admirals*

His parents' warm, comfortable home was constantly filled with children from remote communities—as many as twenty or more at a time. Many of those communities had no high schools, and Gino's mother, Gisele, and his father, Joe, a hard-working and warm-hearted man, always opened their doors to any children who needed a place to call home while finishing their education.

Gino's eyes fill with tears as he recalls the teachings and the love, warmth and support that he and his sisters and foster siblings received growing up. "My dad looked after all of us," says Gino quietly. "His whole life, he worked to take care of us. He went to work in Detroit, New York, working on building the high-rises and bridges, wherever the work was. It didn't matter what the economy was doing, he always found work. There was never a time when any of us were hungry or cold or didn't have good clothes to wear. To this day—he's seventy-three now—he stills looks after his grandchildren the same way."

Joe instilled a strong sense of self-confidence in his only son at an early age, knowing it was a vital form of self-protection for a young First Nations boy struggling with rampant racism in the non-native communities near his home. "Where I grew up in the seventies, coming from the reserve," Gino says reflectively, "I was always treated as a second-class citizen by non-Aboriginal people."

As a kid, Gino played hockey for the reserve team. "We had to stick together because it was really tough. We'd go into town to play the town kids and if we won, we'd need a police escort out of the rink. We were only twelve years old but we needed that protection." Gino's self-confidence helped hold the team together. "I was always proud of the fact that we all stuck together. It was all for one and one for all. We would just form a circle and make it clear that if you touched one of us, you touched all of us, and we weren't going to stand for it."

Gino's dad also told his son never to allow himself to become a victim of the prejudice he faced. "He was sent to residential school and beaten as discipline, just for being who he was, so he knew what he was talking about," Gino says. "I always wanted to prove those people were wrong, that we weren't second-class citizens. My dad approved of that, but he never allowed me to feel sorry for myself. If I was in a situation where someone else was getting the upper hand, he would tease me or joke around with me until I dealt with it. It made me stronger and wiser, able to deal with that kind of situation."

Joe also gave Gino an unparalleled education in dealing with his fears, another lesson that would prove invaluable to him in his hockey career. "He saw that I had a passion for hockey, and he helped me train and build up my strength to play. He really worked me hard. One of the best things I remember that he did was to take me out one day to a mountain nearby our community. It's about four or five kilometres up and across, and we walked up and over it together that first time. It was no big deal. But then around the time of the next full moon, he drove me to the base of the mountain after dark and this time he said, 'You walk across by yourself and I'll pick you up on the other side.'"

Joe didn't let his young son protest or ask any questions. "He just said, 'Do what I tell you.' So off I went. It may have been full-moon time, but the path was in the forest and it was pretty dark. I was nervous about what might be out there, but I made it over okay. When I got to the other side, he was waiting to pick me up. In the truck he turned to me and said, 'Now you keep doing that until you feel comfortable doing it. You just keep doing it until it becomes second nature.'"

Gino did as he was told, crossing that mountain several times more in the dark until he had finally lost all his fear of what might happen to him. "It really helped me later when I started to play professional hockey. I learned by crossing that mountain that it's not what actually happens that drains the energy out of people. It's worrying about what might happen. I remember seeing some of my teammates nervous and pacing around before a game, but I never got pre-game nerves. I never worried about what might happen out on the ice. I always just conserved my energy to focus on what needed to be done, to get through the game and win it."

It was an incredible gift from a father to a young son he knew would need all the help he could get if he was to eventually succeed as a professional hockey player. Gino was big, tough and incredibly strong, but he would still be just fifteen years old when he left his mom, Joe and the rest of the family behind to play minor-league hockey in Montreal. Leaving his family home and community to go to a big city by himself was "about the toughest thing I ever had to do in my life," he recalls.

"I knew it was a huge opportunity for me, but it was very difficult looking back at all those people who supported me—my mom and my sisters, all the people in the community—and just driving away from them like that to go spend my life on the road. They never wavered in supporting me and allowing me to focus on my career."

In 1990, Gino hit the big time professionally when he was drafted into the Vancouver Canucks as a left-winger. He was still only twenty years old. The rest is hockey history: sixty-four goals, seventy-three assists, the fighting nicknames, and his legendary close friendship with Russian superstar Canucks player Pavel Bure, who was drafted a year later than Gino. The two became inseparable, despite their very different backgrounds: "He was a long way from home; so was I. He was very proud of his Russian heritage; I was proud of my heritage; and we were both displaced into this very different cultural environment, so actually we had a lot in common right from the beginning. We're still good friends."

Gino fell in love with the West Coast as soon as he arrived there, even though it was so different from what he had been used to back home. "I loved the mountains. It's such a beautiful place." For a young single man on a good wage, Vancouver also offered an attractive lifestyle that he came to thoroughly enjoy.

"I really liked all the restaurants and the food. Pavel and I would try all these different new restaurants all over Vancouver. It was great. That's still something I like to do," he says enthusiastically. He also quickly came to feel at home. "There were so many First Nations people here. That really helped it feel like a good place for me to be." Within a short time of his arrival in Vancouver, Gino befriended people living on Musqueam First Nation, and he has made his home there ever since.

After finally quitting the NHL in 2002, his decision to stay on the West Coast was easy. The following year Gino, a keen golfer, took on a management role at the Musqueam Golf and Learning Academy at Musqueam's Eaglequest Golf Club.

He felt right at home there too, and not just because the club is on First Nations land. Once again, as in his childhood, he was surrounded by smart, supportive women—and just as he'd done as a teenager, he paid close attention to what they had to say. In 2011 he told Vancouver journalist Jef Choy: "In 2010, Musqueam was voted the most female-friendly course in Canada. We have a woman general manager and assistant general manager, and our head pro is also a woman. It's the secret to our success. The women are the ones who have brought the life into this business. I've learned to just stay out of the way and let them do their thing!"

No longer tied to the demands of an onerous game schedule, Gino looked around for other new ventures. Resting on his laurels simply wasn't an option. Used to the tight and demanding discipline of the professional sports world, he needed to be busy. He also knew he wanted to do something to help other First Nations people enjoy the same kind of success and opportunities that he had—through education, good employment prospects, economic development and greater control over their lands and resources.

"I know what a huge difference it makes to a community to have good businesses up and running and employment for their people, especially the young people. It just changes the whole life of that community for the better. It gives them hope." Gino believes passionately that First Nations people in Canada are entitled to have that hope and that prosperity.

"There's this sign in a band office I saw once, and now it's my mantra: First Nations People Have Always Worked for a Living. The world needs to realize that. The world needs to understand that we will look after Mother Earth properly and keep it safe, but that if we see business opportunities as being consistent with that and good for us we know what to do. We'll do it in the best way, the most environmentally sound way, but we'll use the opportunity to our best

Gino enjoying a visit (with his friend and colleague Peter Leech) to the Nisga'a Lava Beds in northern British Columbia in 2012.
Courtesy Peter Leech

possible advantage at the same time, and we will work very hard to succeed at it."

Over the past decade Gino has put his money where his mouth is, investing in numerous initiatives and partnerships supporting First Nations developments and employment. In 2010 he partnered with Vancouver's Aquilini Investment Group to undertake a six-hundred-unit housing development for the Tsawwassen First Nation in Delta, and in 2011 he began work on an electronic recycling project with the Sumas First Nation in the Fraser Valley.

"They are both very positive projects," Gino says enthusiastically. "That's just the start too. First Nations people know so much, we've been looking after ourselves for so long and doing so much with so little, can you imagine what things will be like when we are all managing our lands and resources again like we used to? Despite all the adversity we've been through, we're still here. We've evolved and we've adapted. I just know in my heart that First Nations are going to dominate the landscape again and when we do, we will do well again here in our lives."

Getting First Nations into business is just one of the ways Gino is trying to improve the outlook for the communities with which he works. He has also become a powerful role model for young First Nations people, joining forces with businessman and youth mentor Peter Leech[3] to run workshops for First Nations kids. In the workshops, Peter and Gino focus on how the kids can conquer their fears, and Gino takes the strong message with him that, like him, they have what it takes to succeed in life.

Three decades after his own childhood battles with racism, Gino is saddened by the fact that First Nations children in Canada still face such struggles. But he wants to turn that challenge into opportunity for the kids he works with and to help them succeed in their goals and dreams. Like his father did before him, he tells the young people: "Don't feel inferior to anyone. You're no better than anyone, but you're certainly no worse. Just do the best that you can every day and give yourselves every opportunity to succeed. Do little things every day to improve, and tell yourself, 'I'm going to make this happen.' It will."

He suggests they each read a good book, and tells them how important reading has been in his life. He also tells them to never forget the importance of their cultural heritage. "It's everything, right? The spirits never lied to me about which direction to go, and how to proceed—to always see the best in people all of the time. You get what you see out of people. I tell the kids, just live with a good heart and a good mind, and just do the best that you can every day. When you live your life that way, even if you lose your discipline a little bit and stray from the Red Path a little, you will always come back. You will learn. You'll have a good life."

3 See "First, I Say My Name is Peter," page 65.

5: First, I Say My Name Is Peter

Agnes asked me, "Who are you?" It was a test, but I didn't know that at the time. I just said, "I'm Peter Leech, I'm from St'at'imc First Nation, near Lillooet." She replied, "No, who *are* you?" I didn't understand. She said to me, "The answer couldn't be simpler, Peter. You're a human being."

Peter Leech, b. 1968

St'at'imc Nation, T'it'q'et Community Village/Musqueam, Vancouver

Former professional hockey player and amateur boxing champion

MBA, economic and administrative consultant

Teacher, youth mentor and role model

Beautiful human being

When asked what's important to him as an Aboriginal person, Peter Leech typically responds: "I'd like everyone to understand who I am as a human being."

That's also how Peter often introduces himself: "First, my name is Peter. I'm a human being." He would be happy if everyone understood not only him, but all of his First Nations brothers and sisters—indeed, anyone from a different culture to their own—in those simple terms.

"An elder whose name was Agnes Peters, a really beautiful woman, was the one who taught me about the importance of understanding each other this way," says Peter, who first met Agnes when he was in his early twenties. "She asked me, 'Who are you?' It was a test, but I didn't know that at the time. I just said, 'I'm Peter Leech, I'm from St'at'imc First Nation, near Lillooet.' She replied, 'No, who *are* you?' I didn't understand. She said to me, 'The answer couldn't be simpler, Peter. You're a human being.'"

Agnes patiently explained to the confused young man: "It's so much easier to understand someone when you just think of them as a human being, instead of being native, or non-native, or Chinese, or Hindu or African-American. Those are labels we put on people. What we are first and foremost are human beings, and it makes it a whole lot easier to understand each other when we realize that."

Peter instantly took her wise words to heart. What she said made a lot of sense. But at the time he was also struggling with the fact that he didn't feel like a particularly wonderful human being. "Back then, I didn't feel very good about myself. I was pretty young but I'd already made a lot of mistakes."

Agnes had the answer to that too. She told Peter bluntly that he wasn't perfect and that he was unlikely to ever be perfect. "She said to me, 'You're a beautiful person, because your life is good, bad, happy, sad, wrong and right.' Over time, she taught me to work on understanding my mistakes, and rather than beating myself up constantly for making them, to learn from them instead. She said doing that makes you a beautiful human being, and she helped me

Peter Leech
Courtesy Peter Leech

to really believe it. Today, thanks to people like Agnes, I love, care for and respect myself as a human being," says Peter. "Today I think I'm a beautiful person."

It's the same message that Peter now gives in the youth workshops that he teaches alongside his business partner and fellow role model, Gino Odjick,[4] the former National Hockey League player. "Agnes always told me that her teachings were gifts that should be given to someone else once I no longer needed them. Today it's her lessons and words that I use when I talk to the kids and young people about their fears and the things that confuse them."

Peter started teaching the workshops in 1994, basing them on a tool he had developed that he called the Wheel of Fear. The tool sets out a simple process for identifying one's fears, figuring out where they come from, and developing effective strategies to overcome them. The Wheel of Fear helps kids deal with such diverse

4 See "First-Class Citizen," page 55.

challenges as public speaking anxiety, bullying situations, serious addictions and mental health issues. "It works really well. It's a tool to help you fix yourself instead of relying on others to fix you, which usually doesn't work. It's a tool that's helped fix me, and I know it's helped many others, both kids and adults."

In his workshops, Peter reminds the kids repeatedly that they are beautiful people, and helps them gain the confidence they need not only to deal with whatever life holds for them, but to succeed in their goals, whatever they may be. "I always tell them, 'You have to be able to understand who you are as a person first and accept that person. When you can love yourself as a person, you can love someone else. When you care for yourself as a person, you can care for another. When you can respect yourself as a person, you can respect another. But it all starts with you as a person. That's the first step.'"

Peter and his workshop partner, Gino Odjick, participate in many community events to promote health and well-being for Aboriginal youth. *Courtesy Peter Leech*

With Gino as his sidekick, drawing in the crowds who want to meet the celebrity hockey player who went by the nickname "the Algonquin Assassin" when he played for the Canucks, Peter has taken his Wheel of Fear into First Nations communities and schools throughout British Columbia. He has also attracted the attention of bodies as distinguished as the World Health Organization, who invited him to be a keynote speaker at their 2007 convention in Vancouver, and of international celebrities like Oprah, who talked glowingly on her television show about how the young man she had recently met had described the concept of personal beauty in the finest terms she had ever heard.

But Peter gets the greatest satisfaction from knowing even one child has benefited from his work. "If I can help just one person's life be better, I can die happy," he says, the emotion thick in his voice. "A few years back, I worked with a thirteen-year-old girl who had entered into a suicide pact with her best friend. The friend died. She didn't. She couldn't talk to anyone about it. I gave her the Wheel of Fear to work with, to use whichever way it could work for her. I told her to take it one day at a time. A few months later she wrote to me to say, 'On this day, I want to thank you.' I wrote back and told her to thank herself for giving herself back her life, for she did all the work. For me, that's what it's all about."

After all these years, Peter has countless stories like that one to tell. One of his favourites is about a young convicted murderer, Stu, who has "I'm a beautiful person" tattooed on his back shoulder. "He was a fifteen-year-old kid in one of my workshops. I remember telling him he was a beautiful person, but I thought he wasn't listening. Then I saw him a few years later in a 'pass-me-by,' and there's this tattoo. I said to him, 'I thought you weren't listening. I thought it went in one ear and out the other.' He said to me, 'I heard every word. I just didn't care at the time. Now I do.' And it's what he is using to make himself a better person and to turn his life around. That's amazing to me," Peter says, with wonder in his voice. "I'm so thankful for it."

That conversation was also yet another important lesson for a man who knows he will never stop learning. "Stu taught me that the kids may not look like they're paying attention, but they hear you. Now I tell that to all the parents and teachers. I know it's frustrating when they talk in class or look like they're not listening. They may not care right now, but they hear you. Someday it will sink in. That's all that matters. Just keep talking to them."

Peter's own childhood was unremarkable in most ways, but it was punctuated by extraordinary events and characters that were highly influential in shaping his adult character and future career path. His father, Walter, was St'at'imc, from the Lillooet area a few hours' drive north of Vancouver. He and Peter's mother, Bernice, who is from Musqueam, were living in Vancouver when Peter was born in 1968. "We all moved back to Lillooet, to my dad's village of T'it'q'et, when I was still pretty small. But when I was seven years old, I was sent back to Vancouver to live with my grandmother at Musqueam."

The little boy didn't understand why he had been sent away from home. "I thought my parents didn't love me anymore, that they didn't want me. Even when I went back home two years later, I still didn't know why I had been sent away. I developed a real fear of abandonment after that." It wasn't until he was twenty-seven that Peter mustered the courage to ask his mother why he had been sent away. The answer was heartbreakingly simple: his grandmother had been in a bad car accident and needed help at home, and Peter was old enough to be useful around the house.

"They thought I wasn't old enough to understand so had never explained the reason to me. I've worked it out now, but it is one of the stories I tell in my workshops—how important it is to understand where your fears come from and to deal with them. I could finally drop my fear of abandonment once I had learned the reason for it and understood I didn't need to have that fear at all. I didn't have to be suspicious that everyone I cared for was going to turn me away eventually."

When he returned to his parents' home in Lillooet in 1977, nine-year-old Peter settled back into school and a sports routine at which he had been showing signs of great promise even before

For Peter, the kids he works with give great meaning to his life. *Courtesy Peter Leech*

leaving for Vancouver. "Ironically, since I am a teacher now," Peter chuckles, "I was *not* a good student academically, right through elementary to high school. Sports were my thing."

Peter had been on skates since the age of four, playing hockey at the local rink. "One of my uncles, Tommy Bull, taught me to skate. He was a very good skater. He was a phenomenal gymnast too. He could have been in the Canadian Olympic team if he had had the kind of support First Nations athletes are getting today." Peter also played soccer, and his father taught Peter his particular passion, boxing. "My dad loved boxing so much. He would never miss one of my boxing matches, but he rarely turned up at a hockey game or at one my soccer games. It was boxing for him, the whole way."

Peter excelled at all three sports, eventually playing soccer at a semi-professional level and winning a gold-medal North American Amateur boxing title in 1984. His father hoped he would become a world-class professional boxer, something that was a realistic ambition for a youngster who had only ever lost one match in his short but intense boxing career. His soccer coaches

Left: Peter, an avid sportsman, played minor-league hockey for several years in his early twenties. While he was also a boxing and soccer star, hockey was always his first love. *Courtesy Peter Leech*

Right: Peter's father, Walter, was a loving and inspirational influence in his life. *Courtesy Peter Leech*

had similar dreams for him. But for Peter, there was only one sport he truly loved: hockey.

"I would spend hours and hours every day, after school, practising," he recalls. "In summer I would put on roller skates and go into the community hall, take in my old eight-track music player, put on Prism or Elvis and just skate and shoot at the net for hours. People would ask my mom what on earth I was up to in there. I was just practising, practising, practising. I loved it."

While his academic studies may have suffered as a result of his single-minded dedication to his sports, at the age of twelve Peter started to receive an extracurricular political education that would leave an indelible impression on him. "My father, Walter, was on the T'it'q'et Council at that time, and he was delegated to attend meetings of the Union of British Columbia Indian Chiefs on behalf of our chief and council. He would take the whole family with him to the meetings. That's when I met George Manuel," he says reverently.

Grand Chief George Manuel, a Secwepemc man from Neskon-lith, east of Kamloops, became the first elected president of the National Indian Brotherhood in 1970. By the time young Peter met him in 1980, Manuel was already widely revered for his political activism and opposition to detrimental government policies and actions toward Canadian Aboriginal people. He was celebrated in First Nations circles for helping to defeat then Prime Minister Pierre Elliott Trudeau's infamous 1969 White Paper, a federal government policy document in which Trudeau had called for assimilation of Indian people into Canadian society.

In the 1974 book *The Fourth World: An Indian Reality*, Manuel and co-author Michael Posluns explored the idea of a new order in which First Nations and other Canadians could peacefully co-exist without losing their culture or identity. The following year, in Port Alberni on Vancouver Island, Manuel presided over the first meeting of the World Council of Indigenous Peoples. Under his leadership the council paved the way to the creation of a document that would eventually become the United Nations Declaration on the Rights of Indigenous Peoples, adopted by Canada in 2010.

By the time Peter sat down with his father in a roomful of delegates at the 1980 UBCIC meeting, this remarkable man—more famous in international circles than in his own country—had also helped persuade the federal government to include recognition of Aboriginal rights in the Canadian Constitution, which would be formally passed into law two years later. Peter, still a child, was unaware of any of this. "All I knew was that George was president of UBCIC. I remember him up at the front of the room, looking around the room, then at me. He said to me, 'You're the only young person in the room. What brings you here?' I told him I came with my dad, but I thought what they were talking about was really interesting."

The conversation quickly became far more than interesting.

The young boy was lit on fire by what he started to hear. "When they talked about the injustices that had occurred, the way First Nations were treated, I wanted to go straight out and burn down the Parliament Buildings! I was so outraged." Older, wiser heads like Manuel convinced Peter to learn more about what had happened so that he could contribute informed ideas toward positive change. "So I started to study the 1763 *Royal Proclamation* [which aimed to regulate trade and settlement in Britain's North American territories] and the 1867 *British North America Act*. Both documents are core to the way in which Canada evolved as a colony. I also learned so much about politics by listening to the chiefs. I didn't really understand it all, of course. I didn't know what I could do. But I certainly understood in my heart that something was really wrong, and it needed fixing."

Manuel recognized a kindred spirit in Peter and took the young boy under his wing. "I would stay with him in the summers at his house in Mission, in the Fraser Valley east of Vancouver. I remember the most amazing people turning up to visit—presidents from Africa, South American heads of state. The president of El Salvador came one day in a limousine surrounded by police cars. They were all there to discuss issues of state with George. That's how well-respected he was."

One morning Manuel told Peter to dress smartly for a visit to a friend of his in Vancouver. "We went into this hotel room there, full of people. When they saw George, this path just opened up between them and there was Pierre Trudeau. I couldn't believe it—his arch-enemy. But George introduced me to him as his friend, the prime minister. That was another lesson to me. They respected each other and could be friends even when they disagreed with each other. And Trudeau really respected George. He gave him a picture that he signed at the bottom: 'To my friend George Manuel, Raging Bull, from Pierre Elliott Trudeau.' He didn't sign it as prime minister, but with his name. He really regarded George as his equal, after everything that George had achieved and fought for. I was so awed by that."

George Manuel was a leader Peter continues to look up to for inspiration and hope for the future.
Courtesy Peter Leech

By the time he turned sixteen, however, Peter had become more focused on his sports than on politics. That year he left Lillooet and moved back into his grandmother's house to finish high school and to look for ways to break into the professional hockey scene. He also kept playing soccer, but more for enjoyment than anything else. Teammate Shawn Atleo[5] quickly became a close friend. "I told Shawn I really wanted to make a run at becoming a professional hockey player, so he decided to be my agent. We were both pretty young and thought it was a great idea! But I think I was his only client ever. He worked really hard, sending out all kinds of mail-outs and trying to get me tryouts."

Perhaps unsurprisingly, Shawn's efforts met with little success. "It wasn't until we met Ronnie Delorme that I finally got some tryouts," laughs Peter. Delorme, a former right-winger for the Vancouver Canucks hockey team and a head amateur hockey scout, befriended the talented young player and helped him get a foot inside the coveted door of the minor hockey leagues.

5 See Foreword, page 8.

Peter would play successfully for both the East Coast Hockey League and the Central Hockey League for the next several years, despite a year of heavy binge-drinking in his early twenties that threatened to destroy his career. His fiancée, Charlene LaRue, was his saviour, telling him to lose the drink or lose her. "I'd never met anyone like Charlene before," recalls Peter. "I had fallen completely in love with her, and I really wanted the relationship to work. So that was it, no more drinking. She's been my rock ever since. We've been married for more than twenty years," he says proudly. "As well as our son, Christophe, we have a daughter, Keanu. Charlene taught me so much about intimacy and relationships," he continues reverently. "I'm a better man today because of my wife."

In 1997, Peter's cousin Andrew told him about a business course being offered by the British Columbia Institute of Technology in Burnaby. Intrigued, Peter enrolled. Despite his previous academic challenges, this time Peter loved what he was studying and excelled. After completing his business degree, Peter started putting his newly acquired knowledge to work as a consultant to First Nations communities, helping them to reorganize their governance institutions and finances for greater efficiency and to position themselves to take advantage of economic opportunities that could provide much-needed revenue to pay for community programs.

These days, Peter likes to stay busy. On top of his consultancy work and running the youth workshops with Gino, he has been toying with the idea of getting involved in the film industry, working with the Katzie First Nation in Vancouver and Aboriginal actor Adam Beach on a potential studio venue. He also teaches intensive business courses at the Nicola Valley Institute of Technology, a role he still marvels at. "Despite getting a degree, I am not a natural academic," he says. "I never thought in my wildest dreams I would ever be a teacher. But I really enjoy it, and the students tell me I am pretty good at it, so that's what counts."

Most of all, he continues to relish the workshops. "I met Gino when he was still playing pro hockey, and I was dabbling in the sports agency business. We really hit it off. I helped him out with a couple of issues and we've been close ever since. Now he's involved with the workshops as well as his other businesses, and it's really great for the kids to meet him and hear his story, hear about the challenges he's been through in his life and realize that they can be successful too if they learn to deal with their fears and care about themselves as people."

The youth, Peter says, have been badly in need of someone to show them the way home. "Somewhere along the way they lost themselves. Not very many of them speak the language. They don't know much about their culture. They don't have a clue who George Manuel was, and that's really sad." That is starting to change, though. "The Idle No More movement really demonstrates that," he observes. "The young people don't want to be stuck in a rut anymore. They want to stand up and have their voices heard, and we need to listen to them, even if we don't always agree with what they say. If we try to shut them up, we'll never hear from them again. We have to listen and support them finding their way home again."

A leadership role in politics isn't completely out of the question, although it's unlikely. "It was my dream once, for sure. I still get people asking me to run for office, but I just don't want that anymore." Peter has helped people like his old buddy Shawn Atleo win national office, and he knows what it takes and how hard it is. "It's just not something I'm interested in now, but you never know." He wishes he still had his father around for good, common-sense advice. "I could always call him and he would just know what to say, what the right thing to do was. Despite all the terrible things that happened to him in his life, residential school and the rest, he overcame all of it. I really miss talking to him since he passed."

A brush with throat cancer in the 1990s keeps Peter keenly aware that whatever he chooses to do, he has to make the most of the time he has. So does a promise he made to George Manuel one night when he was about fourteen years old. "It was two in the morning, and I was in bed," Peter recalls. "George came in and sat down at the end of the bed and woke me up. He asked me to promise him that I would carry on and finish his work if he wasn't able to do it. I was only fourteen, but I promised.

"What I am doing with the youth, helping them to be strong and to succeed, and the work I do in the communities, helping them move forward and hold their own against the governments and achieve their goals, is all part of keeping that promise. If I have to do it one individual at a time, one community at a time and it takes the rest of my life, well, that's how I'll do it."

Thoughts from Bruce Underwood

b. 1969

Chief, Pauquachin First Nation

(interviewed in 2007)

Family—not just my wife, Lila; my son, Landon; daughter, Jessica; and nephew Ambrose, for whom we are legal guardians, but families generally—are what count most to me, both personally and as elected chief of the Pauquachin. My great-grandfather was chief. So was my great-uncle Don, and my uncle Donny. Another uncle, Ken Williams, who was elected to council at the same time I was first elected chief, was also a strong advocate for families. When families are strong, the community is strong; when the community is strong, it can achieve great things.

I passionately believe in bringing up First Nations youth with a strong sense of self-confidence to overcome these problems. It all starts with family. In the village we have the Headstart programs for infants and toddlers, for example—they're challenging their minds, they're eating healthy snacks, the parents are getting involved and learning new skills too. We're bringing language and culture into it too. That's really positive. As a leader, those kinds of things make me happy.

Katherine Palmer Gordon photo

6: The Good Life

If you are defining the good life ... well, I could live on the central coast with a boat and the food would be just fantastic—herring eggs, clams, crabs, fish, other food for trade. It would be the richest life I could possibly imagine, with the best food. I would have fish every day. It's what I'm made of. That would be the good life.

Penny Patricia White, b. 1974
Tsimshian: Kitasoo/Gispaxlo'ots/Gitga'at and Gabriola Island
First biologist, Island Marine Aquatic Working Group
Second biologist, Lower Fraser Fisheries Alliance
Fine art photographer
Loving wife to Tina

The late afternoon sun is streaming through the trees in Penny White's front yard and washing the cluttered table in her living room with light and elongated shadows. Her adopted daughter, Virginia, comes into the room, announces that she has completed the school project she was working on, and sits down at the piano to start practising.

Penny gently shushes her, shooing her out again to go and clean up while we finish talking. As she sits down again, Penny's smart phone buzzes insistently. She can't help momentarily glancing at the texts avalanching into her inbox, but she firmly sets the phone aside and stares thoughtfully out of the window. "One of the reasons I have been able to do whatever I want to do," she says slowly and emphatically, "is because I really respect my native side now. I didn't appreciate how important that was for a long time," she continues. "It wasn't until I was an adult. I finally found my way to that point in my mid-twenties but until then I had been pretty directionless."

Penny White
Courtesy Penny White

In 2001 Penny went to Klemtu, a Kitasoo community on the north coast of British Columbia, to take a fisheries technician job with her First Nation. "It was being there and doing that work that helped me to realize I had an incredibly strong cultural connection there, to the sea and to its resources. They really are part of who I am," she says. "That connection finally helped me realize that my professional path in life should be marine biology so that I could work to protect the resource for my people. It motivated me to go back to school and complete my degree. That was the point in my life when I finally figured it all out.

"The love of my family has also been a very powerful force," Penny adds, smiling at Virginia as, her chores finally complete, the happy little girl runs outside to play with the dog in the warm sunshine. "Too many people miss out on that in our society. It's hard to be whole without it. I couldn't have achieved what I have without the love and support of my family and the whole Klemtu community, helping pay for my education and taking me in as one of their own."

Penny means both her Kitasoo clan and the tight-knit little family she has acquired on Gabriola Island, where she now lives. Penny, at thirty-nine years of age, and her wife, Tina Jones, are the embodiment of what other Canadians might well imagine the epitome of West Coast lifestyles to be.

They are into music. Tina, a founding member of immensely popular children's music band The Kerplunks, is an award-winning composer and Juno-nominated musician who regularly rocks the Gabriola dance floors as well. Penny is a prizewinning photographer. They are both into gardening and growing their own organic food and have acquired several highly productive chickens to augment their diet with fresh daily eggs. They eat mounds of fresh seafood and enjoy nothing more than to hang out at the beach in summer with Virginia and the dog and whoever else cares to join in the fun.

They are a laid-back little British Columbian family enjoying the best Canada has to offer, right on their doorstep. "We have such a good life here together. We've just had our seventh anniversary," beams Penny. "But Tina still looks at me sideways sometimes and asks, 'How on earth did you get to be who you are?' My life has been a bit of a drama show at times," she admits sheepishly. "It wasn't always like this."

Penny's path to cultural self-respect, to being a biologist and well-respected member of the Gabriola community and to living the good life, has been hampered from time to time by some of the classic hurdles that young First Nations people face in Canada: racial discrimination and social stereotyping among them.

She was born in Campbell River when her mother, Lois Georgina White, was very young, and she was brought up in Campbell River by her grandparents, Willard White (Gispaxlo'ots, Gispudwada-KillerWhale) and Gloria White, née Neasloss (Kitasoo, Laxibuu-Wolf). Her Kitasoo grandmother was originally from Klemtu, and her grandfather had also been adopted into the clan.

Penny considers herself extremely fortunate to have been brought up by her grandparents, the people she calls Mom and Dad. Willard passed away in 2011. "My dad was a saint. He was one of the most beautiful, loving, generous people I know. He had a very hard childhood himself but despite that was such a great person. He saved me," she says simply of the man who took baby Penny and her young mother Lois into his arms, and cared for them both. "My mom—my grandmother—was always there for us too. She overcame many of her own struggles after an extremely hard youth. I was so lucky to have them both, and my mother Lois, who is like a beam of sunlight. It is so wonderful just to be near her warm spirit."

But growing up, she had no sense all the same of any strong connection to her extended Klemtu family, and little awareness of the importance of her heritage to her future path in life. "If anything, I think my mom wanted us to grow up just like the other kids in Campbell River, so even though we did visit her relatives in Klemtu sometimes when I was younger and we ate a lot of traditional foods, fish and other seafood, I didn't learn many traditional practices."

Penny with her Gabriola Island family: wife, Tina Jones, and daughter, Virginia.
Courtesy Penny White

On those visits, Penny says, she also always felt a bit out of place. "I loved my family there but I always had a sense or a feeling of not really being from there, that it wasn't my home, which I struggled with." Young as she was, Penny also observed the hardship of life in a remote community like Klemtu, and the legacy of poverty and emotional destruction that colonialism had left in its wake. "Growing up, I just wanted to separate myself from people who were downtrodden. I was living in a non-native world in Campbell River and I didn't understand what really mattered at that age."

School was a mixed bag of experiences. On the one hand, her earliest teachers quickly realized what a remarkably bright child Penny was, especially adept at mathematics and scientific subjects. But in Grade 4, her teacher split the class into two groups, high and low achievers. "He automatically put all the native kids into the low-achiever group," Penny says sombrely. It was incomprehensible to the frustrated nine-year-old, who started acting out in ways she never had before. "I cheated, for example. I would never have done that with a good teacher." Thankfully, that was a

Penny's beloved grandparents, who brought her up and whom she always called Mom and Dad: Willard and Gloria White. *Courtesy Penny White*

short-lived experience. Once she moved on to high school, life was as normal for Penny as that of any other teenager—"Zits, geekiness and a controlling boyfriend!"

As she grew older, however, she also lost even the minimal connection she had previously had to Klemtu, when she started taking on summer jobs and stopped going for visits with her mom and dad. By Grade 11, already in love with science, she had decided she wanted to go to university and focused on getting good grades. Little else mattered at the time to the quiet seventeen-year-old but to get into university, which she succeeded in doing in 1992.

It was bad timing, however. After just one semester, her boyfriend lured her back to Campbell River and things quickly went awry for the young woman. "We broke up—I got really lost for a few years. Things got out of hand in my life," she says quietly. "I did go back to university eventually but got really mediocre grades. I didn't feel any strong direction. So I quit and went to work as a waitress back in Campbell River."

Then, in the summer of 2001, everything changed. "I did a

career test and the whole thing pointed at biology, which required finishing my degree. That's when I got into the university's co-op biology program and got the summer job in Klemtu working as a technician for the Kitasoo fisheries program. I was out on the water all summer. That was it!" Penny recalls: "I loved being up there in a boat so much. It got so I knew where I was without even having to look at the charts. It's the greatest thing—being able to look at the shape of the land, a hill, a stand of trees and know exactly where you are. It was just so beautiful."

Penny had long been fascinated with photography. Willard had given her a camera when she was fourteen, and she had immediately been intrigued by what she could see through the lens. Now she enthusiastically took hundreds of images over the course of the summer, producing some of her best photographs to date. Most importantly of all, she finally started to understand and value her relationship to the area and the connection to her Kitasoo heritage.

Finally Penny knew not only what she wanted but also that she was capable of achieving it. "It was a long time coming," she says. "I was already twenty-seven. But I felt like I could do this. I knew that getting my degree in marine biology and working to protect this precious resource that is part of where I come from and who I am, was not only what I wanted to do, but what I *needed* to do."

She never looked back. By 2004 Penny had a first-class honours double major in biology and environmental studies. "It was really hard work, very strenuous, but I just loved it. I did back-to-back summer courses in Bamfield to finish my degree. I would spend hours and hours in the lab and not get tired."

Each summer, she would work on a fisheries project in a First Nations community somewhere on the West Coast: for Huu-ay-aht in Bamfield, for Penelakut on eastern Vancouver Island, and in the two places to which she felt the greatest connection: Klemtu, and the Gitga'at community of Hartley Bay, on the north-central coast of the province. "Every time I went there it felt like I was returning home at last," she says. "It was absolutely amazing."

It wasn't necessarily easy to apply her newly acquired fisheries knowledge in communities where the collective local resource management wisdom had been acquired and applied over hundreds, if not thousands of years. "The people are so articulate and passionate there about our land and management of our resources. As a young woman coming in with just a BSc, your opinions don't carry a lot of weight. When you are in one of these coastal First Nations communities, there's more than just fish and seafood at stake. There is culture involved. There are social issues, economic factors, business interests and political concerns. It all pointed at having to spend more time to understand it all, and to gain more standing."

Penny was particularly interested in *Porphyra*, a red seaweed growing along the rocky shorelines of the coast and long used by many coastal First Nations (and many other cultures worldwide) as a much-needed and highly valued traditional food source, full of vitamins and nutrients and containing healing qualities.

The community encouraged her to study the seaweed and she readily agreed. Observing how industry had commercialized marine species elsewhere along the coast, Penny understood the community's apprehension at the prospect of similar commercialization of *Porphyra* in Tsimshian territory. "As soon as that happens, the government gets its hands on it and rapes the resource and then it's all gone," she says bluntly. "That's why the thought of commercialization is very scary."

Seaweed, says Penny, is vitally important to anyone interested in sustainable and renewable local food sources, and especially to the First Nations people who are dependent on its availability. "It's one of several cultural keystone species. It's integral to the fabric of Tsimshian culture. The nutrient value is very high, and it was used to trade for clams and oolichan fish grease and for feasts."

Seaweed appears frequently in Penny's detailed, intimate photographic seascapes, and a broad smile appears on her face when she describes how *Porphyra* is prepared and eaten. "There are so many different ways to prepare it! Everyone has their own preference. Some dry it once, others dry it twice. You can squirt clam juice on it. Some people ferment it." Penny likens the level of sophistication of the taste of *Porphyra* to cheese or red wine, both of which she also enjoys: "If you don't understand the taste, you won't appreciate the diversity of it."

She is unstoppable on the subject of traditional seafood resources on the central coast. The passion rings in her voice and shines from her eyes as she leans forward to describe the vastness of riches nestled in the shorelines of her traditional home: not just the fish and crustaceans and shellfish with which we are all familiar, but seaweeds and chitons (molluscs that are vitally important for her people's future cultural well-being).

Colonization has done more than its fair share to constrain the ability of First Nations people to make use of their traditional resources. "Hardly anyone can afford boats anymore, and a lot of knowledge of where the best places to harvest are has been lost. The federal and provincial governments have also taken control away from many of the good places and made it a criminal act to practise traditional management. Fisheries mismanagement by government has also contributed to over-harvesting and putting important species like salmon at risk of extinction," says Penny.

Native people in the past always used methods that ensured the maintenance of abundance, she says, like taking the smaller fish and leaving the largest fish to breed. "That takes great forethought. It is very sustainable and it works. But the federal Indian agents at the turn of the century couldn't bring themselves to believe that First Nations' methods work. They are still only beginning to realize it now."

She says the government is slowly starting to wake up to ecosystem management—looking at the whole circle of species and habitat in combination rather than trying to manage species in isolation, as they have to date—but, she adds with frustration in her voice, "If they had listened to First Nations in the first place we wouldn't have a problem now with sustainability."

Fortunately, she says, what people haven't lost is an understanding and a strong sense of treasuring their local food sources, something she believes will save them in the end. "Safeguarding our local seafood sources is very similar to how small local farmers approach growing food. Here on Gabriola, for example, the local farmers really understand what it takes to grow food sustainably and trade it with the community. Just like us, they know the federal government doesn't get it yet," she says. "They're just too distant from it and listen too closely to the big companies with a lot of money. The more connected local people are to the land and the sea and their resources the better care they take of it, and the better off everyone is."

Living on Gabriola, Penny and her family are fortunate. There is plenty of locally grown, organic food available and the community is devoted to sustainability. But on the island, Penny has a different daily struggle to deal with. "My home is in Kitasoo territory now. My soul is there," she says passionately. "It is very difficult to be so removed from Klemtu and Hartley Bay and the north. We would move there today if I had the choice, but Tina's career connections are all here."

Penny and Tina, who has family in Victoria, were married in 2006. The longer she is on Gabriola, says Penny, the more roots she is putting down. "But I am torn in two," she says. "It's really hard and I don't cope with it well. I can feel myself losing the connection with people and with place. When I am up there, I feel like I am breathing whole, and the landscape feels like it is embracing me. It feels like where I am supposed to be."

But she is—at least, for now—on Gabriola, where she holds on tight to the love of her family there. As a self-employed consultant, she also works as much as possible in the north, holding on to the dream of moving to the central coast one day and closing the circle of her reconnection to her Tsimshian roots. "I could live in Hartley Bay with a boat and the food would be just fantastic—herring eggs, clams, crabs, fish, and other seafood for trade," she sighs. "It would be the richest life I could possibly imagine, with the best food. I would have fish every day. It's what I'm made of. That would be the good life."

In the meantime, Penny satisfies herself that she has at least found her true path at last, working in marine biology and with her people. "My work is related to fisheries but it also involves a lot of community capacity-building and youth outreach, and I do science liaison as well—translating scientific jargon into language that you don't have to have a biology degree to be able to understand. That's so important. As Albert Einstein said, if you can't explain it simply, you don't understand it well enough!"

These days, Penny understands very well what she wants, and she is working determinedly to achieve it. Life is good now, she says, even if some of her goals—like returning to Klemtu permanently—remain a work in progress.

"Even though I am living on Gabriola Island, you could say I have actually come home at last, in my heart anyway. It's a good and welcoming place to be. In the meantime, it's a good life here too," she says, smiling as Virginia and Tina come inside together, hand in hand. "I'm happy."

7: Just Doing It

I think the 2010 Olympic and Paralympic Winter Games was a great accelerator of relationships between Aboriginal and non-Aboriginal Canadians in this country.

Tewanee Joseph, b. 1972

Squamish Nation/Maori, Aotearoa (New Zealand)

North Vancouver

Former executive director and CEO, Four Host First Nations Secretariat, 2010 Olympic and Paralympic Winter Games

Communications and marketing consultant

Lead singer for the Vancouver rock band Bitterly Divine

Board member, Nike N7 Fund

Lacrosse fanatic

Tewanee Joseph isn't exactly sure why he has always felt he has to rush to get things done. "Maybe," he muses, "it's because at one time I thought I would only have a short life. I really believed that I had to cram everything in as soon as I could. If there was something to be done, I just had to do it, and do it right then, as quickly as possible."

He's over that idea, but old habits die hard all the same. He remains a man in constant motion. This guy still has stuff to get done. He even speaks so fast it's hard to keep up. It's been that way, he says, since he was a kid.

The story of Tewanee's birth is an age-old one, as romantic in its own way as it is a little sad. His mother was a beautiful young Squamish woman who won the 1970 Indian Princess of Canada title. His father was a musician in a touring Maori rock 'n' roll show band. In 1971 the band stopped briefly in North Vancouver for a gig. His music-loving mother went to the show, and was smitten. Nine months later, in February 1972, Tewanee was born in Lions Gate Hospital; his father was long gone.

Tewanee doesn't feel particularly bereft by that. For one thing, he has an innate pride in his international heritage. For another, he has typically seen the challenges in his life as opportunities to be seized rather than as excuses for failure. His earliest years were spent growing up in East Vancouver with his mom, his Chinese Canadian stepfather, and his half-Chinese, half-Squamish brother. Life was never boring for a young boy with an active curiosity about his surroundings, eager to explore and meet people. "I would wander around the Downtown Eastside constantly back then and I never felt unsafe. There was always something new to see that was different. I was never bored."

When he was thirteen, his mother left his stepfather and moved back to the tiny cabin she had grown up in on Squamish Nation's Mission reserve in North Vancouver. Tewanee moved in with his grandmother, who was living nearby, and enrolled at the local high school. "It was tough moving into the local scene as a teenager," he recalls. "You're the outsider. You have to prove yourself to the

Left: Tewanee Joseph *Courtesy the Four Host First Nations Society*

Right: Tewanee was an adventurous kid who loved sports of all kinds.
Courtesy Tewanee Joseph

bullies." But Tewanee was lucky: he was a big, feisty kid who loved sports. He quickly became a star player on his soccer, basketball and lacrosse teams. "Sports helped me survive the challenges. Holding my own in play earned me the respect of the bullies. They pretty quickly learned to leave me alone," he chuckles.

Lacrosse became a particular passion. Tewanee was still a teenager when he was made captain of the North Shore Indians Lacrosse Club in the West Coast senior league. His team eventually won four national championships. At seventeen he made the Canadian junior team, and five years later represented the Iroquois Nations at the 1994 Commonwealth Games in Victoria.

Tewanee revelled in his success. His favourite sport also became important to him in a way that he hadn't anticipated: "I learned a lot of real-life lessons through lacrosse," he reflects. "I learned that hard work and teamwork and commitment are the attributes that I need to be successful in anything I do, whether it's sports, business, or in my relationships. That's been proven to me again and again through my life."

But like most typical teenagers, at seventeen he wasn't thinking very much about business or relationships. Sports consumed most of his time. For the most part he enjoyed school, and he planned to further his education, but he had not given that a great deal of thought either. Then, in his last year of high school in 1989, he had an opportunity to take a lacrosse scholarship at an American university. He enrolled for a business degree, and prepared to head south.

Fate had other ideas, however. The same summer, Tewanee attended a youth conference at which legendary Squamish statesman Chief Joe Mathias was a speaker. Mathias was famous for his knowledge, vision and eloquence about Aboriginal rights and title, and what he had to say enthralled his young listener. "I heard him speak about the great conspiracy of the *Indian Act* against the First Nations in Canada," he recalls. Unfairness has always been a big motivator for Tewanee. "The injustices he spoke about made me so angry that he inspired me to do something about it. That meant staying here. There was no way I could leave." In typical fashion, Tewanee didn't hesitate. He gave up his scholarship and instead of packing his bags for the United States, enrolled in a business program at Capilano College in North Vancouver.

The self-confident young man also launched himself onto the public-speaking circuit, holding forth on First Nations rights and treaty issues to any group that showed an interest in what he had to say. He'd already had plenty of practice. "At high school, when some treaty issue was in the news, the local media would often come around to the school and ask for an opinion from the students. Let's just say I was never shy about talking to them!" With his increasing profile as a self-assured and knowledgeable young speaker, one thing inevitably led to another. "I just started to receive more and more invitations to speak as people got to know me, and it went from there."

His own First Nation was also watching him closely. "When

the Mohawk were protesting the development of traditional lands for a golf course at Oka, Quebec, back in 1990," recalls Tewanee, "I was asked to give a youth perspective to a gathering at the longhouse. The chiefs and elders were all there, keeping an eye out on who might be coming up the path for leadership one day." He was still just twenty-one years old, in the fall of 1993, when those same chiefs and elders turned to Tewanee and asked him to run for Squamish Nation Council. Once again, he didn't hesitate.

"The time was right. I had transferred to Simon Fraser University the previous year to carry on my business courses, and I'd had a terrible year there. I failed most of my courses. It was just a spectacularly bad year. I was trying to do too much." At the end of the academic year, he had been offered an out: a chance to do some contract work over the summer for the Nation, developing policies and job descriptions for several reserve-based businesses. "Then I was asked to run for council, and I agreed straight away."

As the elections approached that December, he started knocking on doors in the community, making his pitch for votes. Earnest, idealistic and enthusiastic, he received a warm reception from almost everyone he visited. His great-uncle Percy Paull had advised him to listen more than he talked, and he'd taken that wise counsel to heart. "That was very good advice," Tewanee says. "I learned so much by listening. I had no idea how vast and complex the issues in the community were." His diligence and commitment paid off: he was elected by a comfortable margin.

The workload was overwhelming, even for someone with Tewanee's capacity for getting things done. As is typical for elected officials in small communities, he was at the beck and call of his constituents. But despite the 24/7 nature of the job, he simply—as usual—picked up the pace, not only with respect to his political duties but on all fronts.

By the time his first term of office was up in 1997, Tewanee was close to completing his business diploma and arts degree and was running two of the reserve businesses, managing combined annual revenues of around three million dollars. He also crammed a busy social calendar into his schedule. His daughter, Melina, was born that year.

He was still actively involved in sports, and participated with gusto in the schmoozing that went along with being both a councillor and a businessman. "I was drinking a lot back then," he admits. "I was still pretty young, and drinking is a big part of the business culture and politics, and playing sports. It was also," he realizes in hindsight, "an escape from all the work and all the issues I had to deal with."

Despite that, Tewanee seemed to thrive on the fast-paced lifestyle he was leading. When Squamish Nation Council elections rolled around at the end of 1997, he decided to run again. "I felt there was still more I could do to make a difference, and the fact is that I was enjoying myself. It wasn't a difficult decision to make." Once again, he comfortably won a seat on council.

Two years later, a life-changing experience set him on the road to his future profession. "In 1999, the Squamish Nation concluded an agreement with the federal government that settled a number of outstanding claims against it. It was a $92.5-million deal, with many complex provisions in it. Because it was so significant, it had to be ratified by the Squamish people through a referendum to be effective." Tewanee and his colleague Krisandra Jacobs were given six weeks to come up with a community communications plan. "We had no idea what we were doing! It was an immense amount of work to get done in that length of time."

But who better to ask to get a job done fast than a young man always in a rush to get everything done, and with a proven track record of doing it well? Tewanee grins. "We did it! An overwhelming majority of the community voted to support the settlement. It's very difficult to achieve that kind of majority with such a significant agreement, but people felt very well informed and we succeeded."

That, he says, remains "a really big moment" in his life, and for more than one reason. He discovered that he had a natural talent for communications, one, as it turned out, that he came by

Tewanee has sometimes felt he is walking in the footsteps of his great-grandfather, Andy Paull, who not only undertook communications for Squamish Nation but who was also an avid lacrosse fan.
Courtesy Tewanee Joseph

legitimately. "I will always remember when Chief Bill Williams showed me a band resolution from the 1920s, when the Squamish Nation was dealing with major issues of the time. My great-grandfather Andy Paull was appointed by chiefs and council to be the media contact for the Squamish Nation! That was an incredible connection for me. It feels like I'm walking in his footprints."

Tewanee rarely walks, however, if he can run. It was mid-2000 when the deal with the federal government was ratified. Building on everything that had been learned from the process, the Squamish Nation established a permanent communications department. But Tewanee didn't take charge of it. Nor, in 2001 when his second term of office expired, did he run again. Riding high on a wave of success and enthusiasm, he decided instead to open his own communications and marketing company.

Determined to succeed, he threw himself into developing his new business. "I quickly realized how much I still had to learn, and I knew how important it was to know and understand every tiny thing about this business," he recalls more than ten years later. "I pulled so many all-nighters reading and working on my writing skills, which were my weakest point. I had to. There was no way I was going to fail."

Tewanee's hard work quickly garnered him some significant clients, including the First Nations Financial Management Board and the Maa-nulth Treaty Society,[6] who needed a communications strategy as they worked toward ratification of their treaty settlement with the government. Tewanee also lured a promising colleague to the business from BC Hydro, a young woman named Rae-Ann White who hailed from the Snuneymuxw First Nation in Nanaimo.

"I'd met Rae-Ann in 2001 at a youth conference. I knew she had all the skills I needed in the business, and I really respected who she was as a person," he says with a smile. There was just a little bit more to the story than that, however. "She also loved lacrosse. I thought she was fantastic!" Rae-Ann went to work for the business in 2002. The couple would eventually marry in 2007. Son Koru was born in 2006; another son, Timohoki, was born in 2008.

Koru and Timohoki weren't even close to being twinkles in Tewanee's eye, however, when another of his "babies" was conceived—this one, a notion so ambitious that anyone less single-minded than Tewanee might have been defeated before even attempting to make it reality. In 2004, British Columbians learned that Vancouver and Whistler—municipalities lying smack in the heart of the traditional territories of the Squamish and three other First Nations—would be hosting the 2010 Olympic and Paralympic Winter Games.

A fire lit itself in Tewanee's soul. Squamish Hereditary Chief Gibby Jacob had been a member of the Vancouver Olympic bid committee, and he invited the excited thirty-two-year-old for coffee at a Tim Hortons outlet in North Vancouver to pitch a proposal. "We discussed the idea for a Four Host First Nations Secretariat. The concept was that First Nations would be an integral part of the event. By being part of it that way, we would foster

6 See "A Short History of the Maa-nulth Treaty," page 170 and "Born to Be Free" page 174.

Tewanee with his family: wife Rae-Ann, daughter Melina, and sons Koru and Timohoki. *Courtesy Tewanee Joseph*

public awareness and respect and at the same time generate some long-term economic opportunities for the First Nations here."

Ambitious doesn't even begin to describe the idea. Different First Nations communities, as is the case with other communities in Canada, often have different agendas. Tewanee would have to do more than get the four host First Nations on side; he would also have to try and generate support from First Nations, Métis and Inuit across the country for participation in an event that had typically excluded indigenous people from its privileged ranks. That hardly seemed possible.

Anyone but Gibby Jacob might have laughed and told Tewanee to go home. But Jacob, a kind, warm and wise man, had known Tewanee since he was a young boy. He had a pretty good idea already regarding what the young man was capable of achieving. "Gibby is so supportive of young people," Tewanee says appreciatively. "He gave me his full backing and arranged for me to meet with the councils of each of the host First Nations to get the process under way."

Even with Tewanee's reputation for getting things done, it took a year just to get the four host First Nations signed up to a mutually agreeable arrangement. There was no money to help at that point. He sank $10,000 of his own savings into the dream, determined to give it his best shot. The biggest struggle was getting the federal and provincial governments on board, but even they eventually fell into line behind the steamroller of his passion and vision.

Much of the rest is history, at least to any Canadian who watched the Games. Over the next six years Tewanee flew repeatedly across the country, negotiating, persuading, and sometimes cajoling prospective participants into line. "I wanted it to be the world's biggest potlatch. I wanted the Aboriginal presence to be so huge that it simply couldn't be ignored—it could never be forgotten. 'Indians everywhere' was our motto." He was the perfect person for the job: someone in a perpetual hurry to get things done was exactly what was needed.

Tewanee, an accomplished public speaker, never wastes an opportunity to talk about the issue of reconciliation between First Nations and other Canadians.
Courtesy David Martin

Tewanee became the go-to guy to solve every problem that came up. "I had the premier calling me. I had federal government ministers calling me. My team and I had to make sure everyone had what they needed, when they needed it, with no mistakes and no delays." He literally ran from meeting to meeting, even pulling his hamstring once in the process. More important than anything was the goal of making a permanent mark on Canadian society: ensuring that no future national event could ever possibly exclude full participation by Aboriginal peoples in Canada. "We wanted to make that the new normal."

He is understandably proud of the results: a groundbreaking two-week-long event, broadcast around the world, in which indigenous people played a starring role. Cultural awareness, he believes, was heightened in an unprecedented way in Canada. "I think it was a great accelerator of relationships between Aboriginal and non-Aboriginal Canadians in this country."

In late 2012, leaning back on a comfortable leather chair in his tidy home office in North Vancouver, dressed casually in jeans and a comfortable sweater—his next appointment is picking up his son from school, so there's no call for a suit and tie today—Tewanee contemplates how he would like to see life unfolding from here on out. He's busy, of course. He has a couple of directorships—he's on the Board of Nike N7, a foundation promoting sports in Aboriginal communities in Canada and the United States, and is vice-chair of the Aboriginal Opportunities Committee with the Vancouver Board of Trade.

He also has plenty of work coming in the door, and doesn't feel any urgent need to chase up more clients. The house is paid for and spending more time with his growing family is far more important to him than amassing more wealth. He's practising slowing down. He plans to investigate his Maori heritage in more depth one day, as his children start getting old enough to appreciate it as well. He has done some research into his background and tracked down the man he believes is his father. One day he'll see about getting in touch.

"I'm playing lacrosse again too, that's a lot of fun, and I'm coaching kids, which I'm really enjoying. The band is working a lot too. We've done more than 250 gigs now, including giving a number of performances at the Olympics. That was fabulous. Having a second CD out is a good feeling too." Tewanee, as it turns out, has inherited his father's musical talent, and is putting it into practice as the lead singer and a songwriter for his homegrown rock band, Bitterly Divine.

The seven-member band touts itself in its publicity as "hard driving, with a swaggering sense of fun." Its first CD was released in 2009. *Dreamwalker*, the second CD, was released in 2013. "The first album was about the human condition. It was full of songs about my teenage angst, growing up alone, that kind of theme. This one, which contains all original music, is entirely based on First Nations themes—pride, anger, social justice, history, the works."

He has no aspiration to run for politics again, despite being much sought after by more than one political group. "I want to keep getting stuff done, and politics isn't the place to achieve that for me," he says. Ultimately, he says, that's what it's about: getting things done.

Maybe one day he'll even stop rushing so much to do it. Tewanee laughs. "Maybe!" Then he glances at the clock, conscious of the time despite himself. "I don't really mind what the future holds, really. So long as it's making a difference, so long as I'm getting stuff done, I'll be happy."

Thoughts from Clarence Louie

b. 1960

Chief, Osoyoos Indian Band

(interviewed in 2004)

I used to have a poster on my office wall with a painted warrior on horseback. It read, Fighting Terrorism Since 1492. It's true. Kids taken to residential schools, smallpox-infested blankets deliberately handed out, bands totally wiped out by disease: non-natives need to understand that history. People say they want to develop relationships with Indians, but how can they do that if they don't know who we are and what happened to us? It's just BS. They ask dumb questions instead like, Why don't you get an education? Why don't you get a job?

If you really want to know, it's about what happens when one society tries to destroy another society. What if China invaded Canada and took your languages away, confined Canadians to reserves, stripped everyone of their culture, their spirituality, their right to control their own lives—then tried to fix the resulting problems with Chinese programs run by Chinese people? There'd be a lot of non-native people who would be messed up. They'd be alcoholics and in jail and on welfare too.

We want to fix ourselves our way, not someone else's. My basic mantra is: make sure you keep your cultural identity. Then if you want to prosper, get an education, work hard and throw everything you can at economic development. Economic power is the path to political power. Greater prosperity for First Nations has to mean greater prosperity for everyone in the long run. I would have thought non-native people would welcome that. In your nice city block, would you want a poor neighbour? Would you want a slum trailer next door with junk all over the yard? Of course not. So what makes sense about keeping native people poor?

Photo courtesy Osoyoos Indian Band Development Corporation

8: Standing on Our Own Two Feet

I have no regrets at all about what my daughters will be inheriting from the Tsawwassen treaty. It was without question the right thing to do. The quality of life is improving for Tsawwassen people, and by the time my girls are grown up, it will be so much better for them than it has been for more than 150 years. They will have no problem standing on their own two feet.

Kim Baird (Kwuntiltunaat), b. 1970
Tsawwassen First Nation
Tsawwassen, Greater Vancouver
Former chief, for several consecutive terms
Former treaty negotiator
Born leader and businesswoman
Proud mom

On a warm June morning in 2007, dozens of Tsawwassen First Nation members crowded into their community hall—a plain, rectangular building on the main street of the community that often doubles as a basketball court and dance venue.

Such lighthearted matters as sports and entertainment weren't on anybody's mind that day, however. Everyone was there to discuss something much more serious: the pros and cons of approving the treaty deal that their chief, Kim Baird, had spent more than a decade negotiating on their behalf with the governments of Canada and British Columbia. It was the first nice weather in a couple of weeks. Kim may well have considered that a good omen when her three-year-old daughter, Amy, and her baby, Sophia, woke her

Kim Baird. *Courtesy Simon Fraser University*

up that morning in their home overlooking Georgia Strait on the tiny Tsawwassen Indian reserve, located on the southern fringes of the City of Delta in British Columbia's Lower Mainland.

The minuscule crescent of swampy, salt-saturated land that Kim calls home is bisected at its southern end by Highway 17 and a long causeway to the bustling BC Ferries terminal linking the mainland to southern Vancouver Island and several Gulf Islands. The gigantic Roberts Bank coal and container terminal, the largest freight hub on the West Coast, lies just to the north; another causeway, this one carrying rail and truck traffic to the port, stretches five kilometres into the ocean in front of the reserve. By 2007, the beaches where Tsawwassen people had swum fifty years before were covered in slimy green mud, and the crabs and shellfish they once feasted upon were all gone—victims of industrial pollution and increasingly stagnant ocean water.

That year, nearly eight million people passed through the middle of the reserve on their way to or from Vancouver Island via Highway 17 and the ferry terminal. When the provincial government originally broke ground in 1958 for the terminal, Kim says, "the first anyone here in the community knew about it was a foreman knocking at the chief's door at six in the morning and asking where they should park the trucks." The new extension of Highway 17 cut the existing reserve in half. There was a longhouse in its path, so government contractors unceremoniously tore it down. Ten years later, construction began one kilometre north of the reserve on the coal port. As had happened with the ferry terminal, Tsawwassen First Nation was not consulted on how that might affect the community.

In July 1999, almost exactly eight years before the community meeting to discuss the proposed treaty deal, Kim had spoken at a public meeting in Delta about the First Nation's vision for a treaty. "Our spirit is low," she began. The traditional language spoken by Tsawwassen people was almost gone. Alcohol, drugs and unemployment had taken its place on the reserve. As with other Aboriginal people in British Columbia, life expectancy was far lower than the average for the province and health problems, suicide rates and alcohol-related deaths were as much as five times higher.

More than 50 percent of Tsawwassen members living on the reserve had not graduated from high school. The unemployment rate was 36 percent, and forty families in the tiny community depended on meagre social assistance of $1,000 a month or less. Of those employed, more than half were working off-reserve and therefore paying taxes. The average annual income was under $25,000. By comparison, people living in next-door Delta were employed, well-housed and prosperous, said Kim. "How," she asked the shocked and silent audience, "can the Tsawwassen First Nation find a future that represents the lifestyle enjoyed by the rest of British Columbians and Canadians?"

Eight years later, the First Nation community was contemplating a deal that, apart from settling more than 150 years of outstanding grievances against the governments, might just represent a bright future: an agreement that would provide the Tsawwassen First Nation with badly needed land and income, and restore to them self-government authority and rights that had long been missing in action, subsumed by the *Indian Act* and the legacies of colonialism.[7] The self-government aspect was perhaps the most important aspect of all. If they could take back control of their own lives, Kim believed with all her heart, Tsawwassen people would once again be able to stand on their own two feet as a community, free of the shackles of dependency that the federal government had placed on them so long ago.

All the same, there were people in the room that day with serious doubts about whether the proposed agreement was a good deal. Anti-treaty activists from other First Nation communities had come to the meeting to argue against it. The balance of opinion hung in the air as those present hotly debated the merits of proceeding with the agreement that their chief had struck. What if it wasn't enough? What if they failed to achieve their hopes for

7 See "What's in the Tsawwassen Treaty," page 118, and "A Short History of the Maa-nulth Treaty," page 170.

the future? After all, they had little to go by to judge the agreement against. No other First Nation in Canada had entered into a modern, urban-based treaty of this kind with the government. If they approved it, the Tsawwassen First Nation was taking a leap into new and unproved territory—and every other First Nation in the province was watching closely.

Kim stepped up to the microphone, and the room stilled as she began to speak. "It takes courage to be the first," she acknowledged. "Will we make mistakes?" she asked her people. "Of course we will. That's human nature. But I believe that we are resilient as Aboriginal people, and that we have withstood the worst already." Kim urged the people in the room to say yes to the agreement: "It won't provide us with utopia, or anything close to it," she told them bluntly. "But a treaty *will* provide us with the tools we need to begin rebuilding our community."

In conclusion, she acknowledged that people fear this kind of change. "They are afraid that once we are in charge of our own affairs, we could make things worse. But I trust anyone in this community over anyone from the federal government, any day. I trust and believe in ourselves. I hope we do this, because I want to stop identifying problems and get on with solving them for a change. We have a huge decision to make. It is scary to take a risk, but rewards don't come without a risk. It *does* take courage to be the first."

Kim had no idea whether her words would have the effect she hoped, but just one month later, Tsawwassen members approved the agreement. The provincial and federal governments approved it later that year. The treaty came into effect on April 3, 2009, fifteen years after Kim and her team had started negotiations, and ninety-four years after her great-grandfather, Harry Joe, had first approached the government formally (in 1915) to ask for more land and redress for his people's suffering.

Harry Joe might not have recognized much in the agreement, a twenty-first-century deal for a modern, urban First Nation: no beads and blankets, no more Indian reserve, no more *Indian Act* government, no more tax exemption.[8] Among other things, it provided Tsawwassen with sufficient capital to tackle the social problems that Kim had so vividly described. If invested wisely, the projected revenue stream would make Tsawwassen financially self-sufficient within a decade. The treaty was groundbreaking and unique for its time. It has also rightly become synonymous with the name of the woman who battled for so long with government negotiators to bring the agreement home: Kim Baird.

Many would have considered the obstacles insurmountable: governmental intransigence; horrific racism in neighbouring communities; and strident opposition from highly influential local government, agricultural advocacy groups and commercial fisheries organizations. Kim and the team of loyal negotiators who surrounded and supported her at every step could have easily given up. But anyone who knew Kim also knew that was unlikely to ever happen. In a way, what she desperately wanted for her community was simply what she was always determined she would have for herself: the ability to stand on her own two feet, look after herself and her own needs, and be completely independent.

"I *am* fiercely independent," she agrees. "Growing up, I saw so many women, including my own mother, who were trapped in bad situations, usually for economic reasons. They depended on financial support from people who weren't good for them. So I have always made sure as an adult that I am able to stand on my own two feet financially and in every other way. That's fundamental for me."

Kim was fifteen years old when she moved to Tsawwassen in 1986. Until then, life had been a constant series of shifts around different parts of Vancouver. "I must have been to nine different schools by the time I was in tenth grade," she recalls. Her mother, Edith, separated from Kim's non-Aboriginal father when Kim was seven. Her beloved dad, Lorne, died a year later, and Kim and her four brothers found themselves constantly on the move as Edith tried unsuccessfully to cope financially.

8 See "What's in the Tsawwassen Treaty," page 118.

Then, in 1985, Bill C-31 passed, amending the *Indian Act* and changing the lives of tens of thousands of Aboriginal women and children across the country overnight. Before the amendment, Aboriginal women like Edith who had married non-Aboriginal men had lost their Indian status under the act, as had their children. The same provisions had not however applied to Aboriginal men who married non-Aboriginal women, or to their children. Finally, the discriminatory provisions were gone, and equality of rights restored. Edith immediately applied to regain status for herself and her kids and returned home to Tsawwassen, squeezing her family into a vacant trailer on the reserve.

Despite coming home, the family did not experience much improvement in their lives. "In a way that was an even more difficult transition," Kim recalls. "It wasn't a very happy place back then. There was very little money and plenty of hopelessness. It was pretty sad." It was also a pretty hostile place. Kim and her mother and brothers faced a problem that women and children all over the country were experiencing as they went back to their home communities: reserves simmering with resentment against newcomers. "There was a lot of animosity toward kids like me who hadn't grown up in the community, and it showed."

School life wasn't great either. "I also had to enrol at a new high school in Delta, and I didn't know anyone there. I felt really displaced. I had been an honours student until then, but I was angry at my situation and lost interest in being in school. I barely passed anything." It may not have helped that Kim was in her teenage Goth phase at that point: spiky big hair, heavy black makeup, and a penchant for horror fiction and the dark lyrics of musicians like Nina Hagen and Bauhaus were no doubt off-putting to many of her classmates. "That was quite the look, all right," she chuckles in fond recollection.

Kim credits her three older brothers for "toughening me up" to withstand the challenges. "They were very protective of me, especially after my dad died. I always felt very sorry for any boy I dated, because they always had to deal with my intimidating big brothers hovering in the background!" But not many of those boyfriends made it to her home to actually meet her brothers. "Even my old friends weren't allowed to associate with me anymore, now that I was living on an Indian reserve. Their parents didn't want them hanging out 'in a place like that.' It was a terrible time for me."

It was also highly motivational for the unhappy young woman, however. "I could see the huge difference between this community and the affluent suburbs of Delta and Vancouver. It made me really angry, and I wanted to understand why things were that way. I wanted to find out how we could change that situation and have a prosperous and healthy community as well." After graduating from high school, Kim enrolled in history and political studies at nearby Kwantlen College to study colonial history and its impacts on First Nations people. "Actually I took every subject you can think of with 'ology' at the end of it," she says. "I wanted to learn as much as I could and it didn't really matter what at that point."

In the course of her studies, she learned that the federal government was engaged in comprehensive land claims negotiations with the Nisga'a Nation in northern British Columbia. Not long after that, in 1991, the province finally bowed to long-standing pressure from First Nations to join in the negotiations. A tripartite claims task force was struck to make recommendations on a negotiations process with both governments in which every First Nation in British Columbia could choose to participate. The new treaty process would aim specifically to redress the historic injustices that had led to the kinds of negative outcomes Kim was witnessing on the reserve: poverty, bad health, addictive behaviour and, worst of all, complete disbelief that anything could change for the better.

"My social and political consciousness really woke up, and I started to think that in fact, change truly *was* possible. I was so angry about what I was learning in school, but I wanted to direct that anger toward making change happen. That's when I decided I wanted to work for my First Nation in this new treaty process." Still just twenty years old, Kim volunteered to create a Tsawwassen land claims research department and budget and successfully pitched the idea to her chief and council, initially on a pilot basis.

Kim applied for one of the two positions that had been created in the new department, then juggled her studies with her work until she graduated with her arts diploma in 1992. A year later she was elected to Tsawwassen Council for the first time, and Tsawwassen formally entered into the new BC treaty process. The land claims research department was no longer a small pilot program, but a fully fledged negotiations team.

In 1999, at the urging of outgoing Chief Sharon Bowcott, Kim ran for the leadership position and won handily. It was a big year for her: on top of taking on the enormous role of chief and all the administrative duties that went along with it, she became the chief negotiator for her First Nation, and worked day and night with her team in intense discussions with the government negotiators. It was difficult, occasionally nightmarish and always challenging. But it was also immensely exciting to be at the forefront of groundbreaking treaty negotiations. "I was still only twenty-eight, and was recently single after a five-year relationship, with no kids," she recalls. "I was able to devote myself 100 percent to the work without having to think about anyone else."

Well, perhaps 99.9 percent: footloose and fancy-free, Kim could hang out with her friends in her rare moments of downtime, enjoying a glass of pinot noir at a hip local bar or going shopping to replace a pair of her worn-out but beloved leopard-skin-patterned flats. Even at work, there were moments, infrequent as they were, when she was just plain having fun. Former colleagues and friends alike fondly recall the image of Kim flying down Highway 17, heading to a meeting in her white soft-top convertible sports car, her shock of black curls flying in the wind, a latte steaming fragrantly in the cup holder, one hand on the wheel (most of the time), and laughing her big, hearty laugh into her cellphone while flipping through her scheduler.

"Those days are *long* gone," she says primly, albeit with a hint of nostalgia in her voice. That's because 1999 was a big year on the personal front too. That's the year she met Québécois carpenter Steeve Lachance, in an argument over Aboriginal rights in a local pub. "Poor Steeve—he was just as intimidated by my brothers at the beginning as any of my teenage boyfriends used to be!" Kim laughs. Her French capabilities were equally tested on her first trip to Quebec. "That was daunting! I didn't speak any French and they spoke very little English." At her first Christmas with Steeve's family, she was served traditional Quebec Christmas fare. "We had tourtière, and other French dishes. There was no salmon, which I was used to having at Christmas. It was all quite foreign to me." Steeve's family were equally bemused to be sitting down to dinner with a First Nations chief as their future daughter-in-law. "But it all was good," Kim says. "They really loved becoming grandparents eventually."

In 2003, Kim's first daughter, Amy, was born. The convertible was traded in for a utilitarian and road-safe van equipped with a child's car seat, and the days of multitasking en route to a meeting, latte and/or cellphone in hand, were over. Now work duties also

Kim with her daughters Amy, Sophia and Naomi, 2012.
Cherryl Willliams photo

had to be juggled with being a mother. In typical style, it never occurred to Kim that her children would not simply become part of her work routine. "I just brought Amy with me to the office, and to negotiations meetings. Everyone was fine with it. A woman recently told me I broke a glass ceiling when I did that. But I didn't even think about that. I just never thought I *couldn't* do it."

In the meantime, Kim continued with her education on the side. It was feasible to think that, one day in the foreseeable future, the negotiations would finally be over. Kim wanted to be prepared to move on to the next phase of her career, so had enrolled at the University of British Columbia to study geography and sociology. Her second daughter, Sophie, was born in 2006, during the throes of final negotiations. Naomi came along three years later. Like Amy before them, the younger girls accompanied their mother to work and meetings, and even to the floor of the Legislature.

In October 2007, as the provincial government considered the legislation that would make the Tsawwassen treaty reality at last, Kim and her little girls watched anxiously from the public gallery above until the final overwhelming vote in favour of the treaty was taken. In honour of the treaty's passage into law, Kim was invited to speak to the Legislature from the floor—the first non-elected woman to be given the honour in British Columbia. By her side, naturally, were the girls, who are members of the first generation born to Tsawwassen who will grow up in the post-treaty world that their mother envisioned when she first started working toward that goal so long ago.

Kim and Steeve are no longer a couple, but their beautiful daughters are the light of their mother's life. "I am so proud of my children," she says quietly. "I know it sounds hokey, but everything I went through was worthwhile because of them. I have no regrets at all about what they will be inheriting from the treaty," she continues. "I don't lose sleep anymore about whether or not it was the right thing to do. It was without question the right thing to do. Some people questioned my judgment at the time. They said I was so young, I didn't really know what I was doing. Well, there's only

Top: In 2007, Kim became the first non-elected woman invited to speak in the British Columbia Legislature, after the passage into law of the Tsawwassen treaty legislation. © *2013, Province of British Columbia*

Above: Sitting alongside federal and provincial cabinet ministers, Chief Kim Baird signs the historic Final Tsawwassen Agreement in Ottawa, in 2007, on behalf of Tsawwassen First Nation. Witnessing the signing is Laura Cassidy, a Tsawwassen councillor and long-standing member of the Tsawwassen negotiations team. *Courtesy Tsawwassen First Nation*

one answer to that—to prove them wrong. I think the results are proving them wrong already. The quality of life is improving for Tsawwassen people, and by the time my girls are grown up, it will be so much better for them than it has been for more than a century. They will have no problem standing on their own two feet."

One thing Kim has had to learn to accept is that while signing up to the treaty was the right thing to do, it didn't necessarily put to rest all the anger she had felt for so many years over the injustices her people had faced. "I think there will be reasons to be angry for a long time to come yet," she reflects. "There are still wrongs being done every day to First Nations people in Canada, and that saddens me. But I also have learned how important it is to put the past behind us now and look to the future. We must never forget our history, and I'm teaching my girls that. But we must also look forward to make sure that we never allow that to happen again. That's very key to our future success, and a very powerful way to achieve it."

As to her own future, Kim is confident. Although she is no longer chief of Tsawwassen, playing that role throughout the years of negotiating and implementing the treaty was an extraordinary experience. It was never a role she saw herself in for the long term. As she pointed out in April 2013, with a mischievous and determined glint in her dark eyes, "I suspect I'm highly employable."

Indeed she is. Her résumé of achievements runs to several pages, with numerous awards starting to pile up on her desk. In 2012 she won a Distinguished Alumni Award from her original alma mater, Kwantlen College, for community and public service. She is also a recipient of Canada's Top Forty Under 40 Award, the National Aboriginal Women in Leadership Distinction Award, *Vancouver Magazine*'s Power 50 Award, Canada's Most Powerful Women: Top 100 Award, and an honorary doctorate from Simon Fraser University.

Kim has also been on the board of directors of BC Hydro, Metro Vancouver, and several First Nations business, employment and skills-training organizations. She is in big demand as a speaker, not only in Canada but as far afield as Venezuela, New Zealand, Hong Kong and Dubai. The world is pretty much Kim's oyster these days: it isn't so much a matter of wondering what she *could* do out in the world, it's more a matter of which one of many attractive options she should seriously consider. "It's not a bad problem to have," she admits, laughing.

But first things first. On the personal front, she says: "I would like to spend more time with my children. I would love to get back to school and complete my studies. For fun, I like pottery, and I love writing. When I was ten years old, I wanted to be an author, and I still do. I would like to explore that further. I'm a perfectionist, so I definitely have to get over that, but at least I know that about myself!"

She may even write about her own experiences one day. "There are so many First Nations that are coming to us now and asking for help, asking how we did what we did. I get a lot of young Aboriginal women approaching me and telling me they have been inspired by my achievements, and that seeing my work has made them want to do big things in their lives too. That is such an honour, it makes all the hard times just vanish into the past when I hear that. I hope I can continue to be a mentor to young Aboriginal women and men to help them with their dreams and goals."

One message she will always give them is a reminder that in the end, just like she did, and as her community is doing now, they will have to stand on their own two feet. "Being able to do things for yourself, having to work to get what you want—that's so important. If it is handed to you on a plate, you will never understand the true value of what you have."

It's a lesson she is instilling firmly in her daughters as they grow up. She wants nothing but the best for them, as she does for every other First Nation child of their generation: to make sure they have the kind of childhood every Canadian child deserves, full of love and self-confidence and cultural strength, comprehending but never actually experiencing the hardships their ancestors faced. She wants them to understand they have to work toward that in their own right, to earn a successful and independent future on their own, just as she has done. No one is going to hand it to them on a plate.

Meanwhile, if Kim's original vision holds true, any remaining fears that the Tsawwassen First Nation people have about their treaty will fade away as time passes. Their future is finally in their own hands, and it appears to be one of enormous promise. The next generation, including Kim's daughters, will indeed be enjoying an independence their forebears have not known for more than 130 years.

"This isn't just about money," she told her people at that long-ago meeting back in 2007. "It's about moving forward and putting the long, sad chapter of poverty and dependency behind us, and leaving a legacy for our children and grandchildren for a far better future. It's in our hands. We must do this. We must stand on our own two feet."

What's in the Tsawwassen Treaty

The 2009 Tsawwassen agreement provided, among other things, for 334 hectares of land to be added to Tsawwassen's existing reserve. The land became fee simple, like other Canadian privately held land, no longer an Indian reserve or subject to the *Indian Act*. Decisions on land use would no longer be subject to the veto of a federal government cabinet minister, and property owners were entitled for the first time to sell their own land and raise mortgage financing, something that had been almost impossible until that time.

The removal of Indian reserve status means that all provincial government laws applied on Tsawwassen land for the first time. Accepting BC government jurisdiction was a difficult provision to swallow, given the history of indifference that the provincial government had shown to First Nations people until recent years, but it was a two-way street: in return, Tsawwassen assumed a role in provincial land, cultural heritage and environmental management issues in the region.

Tsawwassen now has its own government with jurisdiction over its lands, somewhat like a municipality with the authority to make bylaws and the responsibility to be financially accountable. It has become a member of the Metro Vancouver Regional District and participates in regional municipal governance in that capacity. Unlike municipalities, however, the new Tsawwassen government is able to make laws relating to cultural, health and educational matters of importance to the people, such as language preservation.

On any other matter that is not purely an internal issue for Tsawwassen (for example, the internal distribution of fishing licences), local laws are subject to the laws of Canada and British Columbia. In all cases, Tsawwassen bylaws must comply with the Canadian Constitution. In other words, no sovereign nation has been created (and no part of the sky has fallen in as a result).

The federal government transferred cash totalling about $20.7 million—sufficient to tackle the social problems that Kim Baird experienced as a teenager and young adult—to the new Tsawwassen government. So long as Tsawwassen continues to invest that money wisely, its financial advisers have calculated that combined with their own income from various sources, that capital sum will make Tsawwassen financially self-sufficient by 2021, and earning ten times the annual revenue it used to receive from the federal government's old department of Indian affairs.

Tsawwassen also receives ongoing transfer payments from the federal government to fund programs and services for residents living in Tsawwassen's jurisdiction (similar to the transfer funds municipalities receive each year from government to carry out their functions). Also like municipalities, Tsawwassen contributes its own revenues to its annual budget.

In 2017, Tsawwassen people will have to pay sales taxes; in 2021, income taxes. Tsawwassen will also be able to levy taxes on its own members, such as property tax. For Tsawwassen people not living on the reserve, that change will have little impact, as they are already paying these taxes. The transition period is intended to allow those who have been living and working on the reserve time to adjust. As reserve resident and former Tsawwassen councillor Remo Williams pointed out at the time the treaty came into effect, if he starts paying taxes at least it means he's earning income: "My exposure to the wonderful world of taxes is that the 'haves' always find loopholes that work for them, so hopefully we'll start getting some 'haves' right here in Tsawwassen."

9: We Will Go Forward

Despite all these dark truths—so many First Nations kids in care, the highest suicide rates in Canada, communities with very little infrastructure—we can still smile, laugh and tell stories, and can pass on the teachings that existed before all this happened. There are all these vibrant, positive people who have resilience, who want to go forward and who will go forward. That's what matters when people talk about bridging the gaps.

William "Bill" Yoachim (Sqwulutsutun), b. 1970
Snuneymuxw First Nation
Nanaimo
Band councillor
Double BA, First Nations studies, social work
Executive director, Kw'umut Lelum Child and Family Services
Member, Vancouver Island University Board of Governors
Passionate advocate for change

On February 19 every year, William Yoachim mourns the passing of his beloved mother, Ivy, who took her own life on that day in 2000. The grief at her loss will always be with him. But although it was impossible to see it at the time, Ivy's son later realized that her passing was also transformational for him.

"Every day I wish my mom was here with me," William says, the ache of her loss audible in his voice. "But the day she died was also the day that I was forced to start thinking about who I am. It was the day I really became involved in the concept of working for my people. I have never looked back."

William, who is known as Bill, grew up in suburban Nanaimo on Vancouver Island, an ordinary young boy whose German father worked as a welder on gas pipelines in the North while Ivy raised her son and his older sister, Terri. Having Indian status or not was of little account to him then. Like the other kids, he played soccer, went to the local high school with all his friends (both Aboriginal and non-Aboriginal), and hung out with his Snuneymuxw grandparents and relatives on weekends.

William "Bill" Yoachim
Courtesy Dean Kalyan Photography

"I was brought up off-reserve, but I never knew the difference then—I had no idea what that meant. I was accepted in both communities and having Indian status or not didn't make a difference in either one." Bill considers himself fortunate: "I was lucky, I know, because I have seen the impact it's had on some people who faced discrimination off the reserve or who were shut out of the community because they *weren't* living on the reserve or didn't have a status card. I never had either experience."

Bill spent his early adult years working on the northern British Columbia and Alberta pipelines, like his father before him. "I never envisioned obtaining a post-secondary education at that time," he recalls. "It never even crossed my mind." But in 1997, encouraged by his family—especially his aunt Joyce White, who was running the First Nations studies program at Malaspina University-College in Nanaimo—he decided to give it a try, and enrolled in her courses.

Bill received his first bachelor of arts degree, in First Nations studies, in 2004. He immediately enrolled for his second degree, this time in social work. In 2007 he took over as executive director of Kw'umut Lelum, a First Nations-operated child and family service agency serving nine First Nations on southern Vancouver Island. In July 2008, he was appointed to the board of governors of Vancouver Island University (formerly Malaspina) in Nanaimo, one of the few Aboriginal people in the country to serve in that capacity.

It's a remarkable series of achievements, but Bill has been driven to succeed. His reasons for wanting to become a social worker include his belief in children as the most important guardians of society's future well-being. The fact that he was sexually abused as a child by his soccer coach is another of his motivations. "I don't want this to sound like I'm a victim or make this into a sob story, because it isn't—but it also helps explain who I am now, and why I have ended up doing what I do," he says frankly.

Bill tried to report the abuse at the time it occurred, but was stonewalled by the authorities, his complaints dismissed as unsubstantiated childish statements causing more trouble than they were worth. However, in 1997, after enrolling in school and settling back into his community, Bill summoned the courage to try again, laying formal charges against the man who had done so much damage to him and other children. This time, the man was convicted.

It was one of the hardest things Bill has ever done in his life, but worth it. "I remember the day in May 1997 that I finally went to the police station and told them what had happened, like it was yesterday," he recalls. "I talked to them for several hours, telling them everything. Afterwards, I felt so free. I realized that if I could take control of that situation, I could also take control of other things in my life to improve it." His decision to speak out also encouraged other kids who had been abused to come forward. "So in a way, it was the beginning of this journey to helping other people."

Ivy's passing three years later cemented the path that he was on. The reasons Ivy took her life are hers, and personal; suffice it to say she faced insurmountable challenges. But for Bill, her death was the hardest of all lessons. "I wish I had realized earlier in my life how much Aboriginal women are the most marginalized people in Canadian society," he says. "Now I know how difficult it was for my mother. It still breaks my heart." He faced two choices at the time of her death: "I could get angry and stay angry, which gets you nowhere, or I could make a difference. I decided to make a difference, and go forwards instead of backwards. That was a much more powerful route to follow."

Bill has put a lot of thought into what will make that difference, and how to bridge the gap between Aboriginal people and their fellow British Columbians: what will help remove the barriers that prevent Aboriginal people from going forward. First Nations, including his own community, still struggle with negative social statistics and poverty. Like him, they are ordinary Canadians, living everyday lives in most respects.

But many First Nations people are also living their lives in extraordinary circumstances, dealing with forcible separation from their culture, discrimination because of the colour of their skin, and irrevocable loss of their land. "You take away rights, traditions, the land and the means of self-sustainability—that represents our whole way of life. No wonder we have out-of-control suicide rates, poor health and bad housing. How *do* we move forward from that situation?"

It is a question he grapples with every day, both in his job and as an individual First Nations citizen of Canada. "I have come to realize that a sense of dignity, respect, a strong sense of belonging—all these things are so vital for anyone," he says. "We're very fortunate in this territory because we have such vibrant, resilient people living here, and young people who I can see are ready to take up the challenge as citizens of this twenty-first-century world we live in." It's time, Bill says, "to pay attention" to the flood of bright young Aboriginal men and women growing up in communities all through British Columbia, "take advantage of that energy and intellectual capital and support it. That will benefit everyone."

He says it matters intensely how his people feel about themselves. He recalls a heartbreaking moment many years ago, when he was bringing a group of Snuneymuxw kids back home after a sports tournament in Victoria. As the school bus turned onto the reserve, one ten-year-old stared sadly out the window and said to him, "It sucks to be back here, man." His heart heavy, Bill knew that he had to keep working to help people feel better about the place they lived—and to recognize their own inner strength, as individuals and culturally.

"Despite all these dark truths—so many First Nations kids in care, the highest suicide rates in Canada, communities with very little infrastructure—we can still smile, laugh and tell stories, and can pass on the teachings that existed before all this happened. There are all these vibrant, positive people who have resilience, who want to go forward and who will go forward. That's what matters when people talk about bridging the gaps."

One thing he would like to see become a thing of the past is the commonly held assumption by non-Aboriginal people that First Nations have all kinds of advantages under the *Indian Act*. "Those

In 2013, the Province of British Columbia signed a reconciliation agreement with the Snuneymuxw First Nation, with the goal of economic benefits for the First Nation and for businesses in the region. Bill Yoachim, a Snuneymuxw First Nation councillor, is pictured seventh from left, standing next to Snuneymuxw Chief Douglas White III (Kwulasultun). *© 2013, Province of British Columbia*

misinformed attitudes really matter. They really hurt us. I have this conversation all the time, everywhere I go—cafés, sports clubs, on the golf course. It's classic. They ask: 'Why are you complaining? You guys get all the breaks.'" But Bill says whatever breaks Aboriginal people get under the *Indian Act* are minor. "Some money for cheap eyeglasses and really minimal funding to help with education. Big deal. Want to trade places?"

Bill tries to hold his frustration in check and answer the questions candidly to get the real facts across: that the *Indian Act* has more limits than benefits; that entrenched poverty breeds diffidence and fear of failure; that 150 years of colonization in British Columbia have done damage that will take as long again to repair; and that First Nations people, like everyone else, simply want a good life, with everything that entails, including physical, spiritual and cultural well-being.

"I find if you just lay it all out on the table, most people start to understand. With understanding you can start building a relationship, and I think that's the best way forward for First Nations now—building relationships with their neighbours so our communities can live together as one, while still respecting each other's rights and differences. It's a much more positive way to go, and it's good for everyone. We all have to go forward, First Nations and non-Aboriginal people alike, and it's a lot easier to do it arm in arm than pushing against each other."

Bill has seen things changing for the better in recent years. "I definitely see positive change happening. We're very fortunate that our teachings have stayed intact. What's happening is that there is more balance now—we are keeping the Indian way, but we're balancing it with Western ways of doing things at the same time. I see that as very positive, as making the best of both worlds." He is particularly cheered when he watches some of the young people he started working with more than ten years ago—including that ten-year-old on the bus—be part of that change. "It makes my day to see them now as confident young people living balanced lives here in this community."

"Keeping the Indian way" is the philosophy that cradles the work he oversees at Kw'umut Lelum. The First Nations agency operates under delegated authority from the provincial government, delivering child and family welfare services to First Nations communities. "It's difficult work, but it's exciting at the same time because while we have to operate within the government system, we're able to do it our way—the way we've been approaching these issues for thousands of years, like using family group conferences to deal with a kid who's acting up. We've always done that this way, since the beginning of time."

That's so much better for the families involved, he believes, than being supervised by non-Aboriginal social workers from the provincial Ministry of Child and Family Development, who know little about the communities or culture of the people in need of help. "We're bringing a First Nations voice and teachings into a practice where First Nations never have had a voice before."

The importance of following First Nations cultural practices cannot be overemphasized. Culture, Bill says, isn't art sold in native galleries in the tourist-populated parts of town or dance shows as paid entertainment: it lies in teachings and tradition, and its value to spiritual well-being cannot be overestimated. "It's a way of life. Everything that's done and said is for a purpose, whether it's a ceremony in the longhouse, or clam-digging. Our cultural identity is in every part of the territory. It's so grand, and so beautiful. It makes us who we are as people. That's why approaching the healing of the children with the teachings of their own culture is so important."

Bill says that according to the statistics, the number of First Nations children who have been through the provincial government's child and family services program is now greater than those who went to residential schools. "That's pretty disturbing, when you consider the damage that the residential schools did."

Dealing with the root problems behind those statistics—poverty, the damage caused by the residential schools, and a host of other cultural crimes against First Nations—is an urgently pressing matter. But until it is resolved, dealing with the children and families in need of help from a First Nations perspective is equally vital. "We know these communities and the particular issues they face. We know the families—they aren't strangers to us. So we can manage the internal challenges with greater flexibility and understanding. Our approach is community-focused, with a much more positive attitude toward resolving the issues."

Positive attitudes toward First Nations governments matter too. Indian band councils often suffer from negative public perceptions, but the vast majority of them juggle huge workloads with relatively little funding and do their utmost to serve their communities well. Support from neighbouring non-Aboriginal community governments can be helpful. Bill cites the work that Snuneymuxw and local governments in Nanaimo (as well as the provincial government) have put into building respectful, positive relationships over the past few years.

The practical benefits of those relationships include co-management agreements and economic development opportunities for the First Nation, allowing it to build its financial independence. Not least of all, for the first time in Nanaimo's history, in 2012 Snuneymuxw communities started to receive badly needed water services—and, in the not-too-distant future, will be getting sewer services as well.

An emotional and spiritual benefit comes, too, from respect for and acknowledgement of his First Nation's cultural identity and right to govern itself in its territory. "With support from our neighbours, I believe the day will eventually come when we really can bridge the gap for Snuneymuxw people and we can all go forward together, community to community, with a common vision that is in everyone's best interests," Bill says.

He also thinks the time has come for First Nations, especially the younger people, to take their turn in helping to bridge the remaining gaps. "They have a job to do now—whether it's as teachers, or like me, taking a role on the board of governors of Vancouver Island University—to share a wealth of knowledge we have on how to make this a better place for everyone."

The university appointment recognizes his energy and work in a way that Bill savours after all the difficult times. "I've had challenges sometimes on band council and in my job," he acknowledges. "But I think about the people who voted for me, or who I am working with. It's hard, but nowhere near as hard as some of the things they've gone through, or that I went through earlier in life. That makes it easier to stay positive and think about doing this for my community, for my ancestors, and for all the marginalized people out there."

In 2006 Bill married Lori Pockiak, a registered nurse working at Nanaimo Regional Hospital. A 2013 Valentine's Day card on one of the bookshelves in his office at Kw'umut Lelum proclaims: "A kiss is just a kiss, a sigh is just a sigh ... but a good loud snore means we're happily married!" Bill reflects with gratitude and love: "I could not have been blessed with a more wonderful supporter than Lori."

Samantha is the apple of her father's eye. Bill is married to Lori, a nurse, and Sammie is their first child.

Courtesy Bill Yoachim

The couple celebrated the birth of their first child in 2009, daughter Samantha. Becoming a father has cemented his belief in taking a positive approach to removing barriers to well-being and moving forward in life as part of a loving, respectful community. "We want to raise her to always be proud of who she is and where she comes from, and to contribute to her community in good ways. We want to make sure she always feels good about coming home to Snuneymuxw territory."

In the meantime, his mother Ivy's influence is never far away. Sitting in his cluttered office surrounded by piles of paper and bulging files, his iPod quietly playing music in the background, photographs of his family on the walls and crayon drawings by Samantha pinned to his notice board, Bill says: "I often ask myself what my mom would do or say in a certain situation, especially when it's really challenging. I think she would simply say we have to go forward. So that's become my philosophy, it's become part of who I am. I want to keep working on removing the barriers, and doing what I can to support my people, the children and the youth, to move forward. I'm going to keep doing that as long as I can, as long as I need to."

10: Aiming Past the Finish Line

When I left my community near Cranbrook to move to Vancouver all those years ago, I needed to prove to myself I could do all these things. I needed to stand on my own two feet and take responsibility. That's what I did, and it's what I'm still doing.

Beverley O'Neil, b. 1965
Ktunaxa Nation, southeast British Columbia
Vancouver
President, marketing and communications company
Marathon runner
Freelance writer
Stand-up comic

The trick to successful marathon running, Beverley O'Neil confides over coffee in a downtown Vancouver café, is not to target the finish line but to visualize going beyond it. "If you only plan to finish, that may be all you accomplish," she says. "Many people believe that goal setting should be within the parameters of what you can reasonably accomplish in a lifetime, but I believe that if you aim past it, then it's just a milestone along the way to limitless other possibilities."

A slender, athletic woman with an irrepressible twinkle in her dark eyes and an enigmatic smile, Beverley has completed more than twenty marathons since 2007, earning her a much-coveted membership in the international Marathon Maniacs organization. It's still early on Saturday morning, but she has already completed a ten-kilometre training run. "It used to feel like a longer distance," she says, "but after running full and half-marathons, now it seems short. Everything is relative. It's all a matter of perspective."

In many ways, her life tends to resemble a marathon that she's still in the course of running. The fact that it's a weekend, for example, isn't going to make much difference to her schedule today. After her coffee, she will head home to write a story or newspaper column, practise a comedy routine, or return to her consulting and marketing company work. She used to work seven days a week for ten or more hours a day. Now Beverley realizes that living a good life requires a balance between work, personal life and rest, but she's still a busy woman. She's happy to be that way.

For more than twenty years, aiming past the finish line has been the goal-setting psychology Beverley has applied to almost every aspect of her life, whether business-related or personal. She studies her route in advance, and for each stage of it carefully plans her strategy, goals and approach. This is her race and no one else's. But as she has also had to do many times in the middle of a long-distance event, from time to time she has needed to adjust her strategy and stride along the way to deal with the inevitable challenges she has encountered en route, and seize the opportunities that have presented themselves.

Beverley posing for *BCBusiness Magazine*'s "Who-What-Wear" page in February 2007, wearing a shawl by Haida fashion designer Dorothy Grant.
Courtesy Peter Holst Photography

Her personal mission statement also focuses on identifying opportunities to push limits aside rather than on finding barriers to success. "Open eyes, open mind, open heart," she intones. "It's simple, yet effective." It's a formula for both professional and personal achievement that's worked well for her: Beverley is a self-described master of her own destiny who has won awards and who enjoys a highly respected reputation in business. She has run her own successful marketing and communications company in Vancouver for more than eighteen years, has had seats on several high-profile boards of directors, and has a substantial portfolio of freelance non-fiction writing projects.

On the personal front, in addition to her athletic activities, she is enjoying a burgeoning sideline as a stand-up comic and is working on a couple of potential fiction book projects. She also owns a comfortable condominium in one of the trendiest neighbourhoods in downtown Vancouver, and a sweet little black BMW convertible that she has affectionately dubbed the "Baby Batmobile" and that suits her independent single lifestyle perfectly.

The material benefits of her hard work are nice, of course, but it's the intangible consequences that have proved the most meaningful to her. "To me, the value of a dollar is what I put into earning it. It's rewarding to see the results of the work I've done, or coming out of something I've created," Beverley says. "At the end of 1994, when I moved to Vancouver [from the Kootenays], I needed to prove to myself I could stand on my own two feet and take responsibility for my career and my business. I call it the symphony of entrepreneurship—you create the music, face the music, and enjoy the music. That's what I did back then, and it's what I'm still doing."

Beverley's father is Irish Canadian. Her mother is a citizen of the St. Mary's Indian Band near Cranbrook, in the heart of Ktunaxa Nation territory in southeastern British Columbia, but Beverley was born and brought up in Windermere, off-reserve, 125 kilometres north of Cranbrook. It was an unremarkable childhood, or as near to it as can be said of living in a household with three older vivacious, energetic and good-looking sisters and a

Left: Beverley has run multiple marathons, and running has become an integral part of her routine and her life. In this image, taken in 2007, she was competing as a member of the Victorious Secrets team in the H2H 100-kilometre relay.
Courtesy Beverley O'Neil

Right: Beverley visits the grave of her grandfather, Toby Nicholas, in the Agira Canadian War Cemetery in Sicily, Italy, in May 2005. It was a chance for Beverley's mother and great-aunt Phyllis to say goodbye at last.
Courtesy Beverley O'Neil

lone, beleaguered young brother. After leaving school, Beverley eventually headed for Edmonton to study business marketing at the Northern Alberta Institution of Technology. Within a couple years, however, she was back in the Kootenays, this time on her mom's home turf near Cranbrook.

In 1990, with her business diploma in hand, she had just been offered a marketing job with the Edmonton professional soccer team when the opportunity arose to relocate to the St. Mary's Indian Band to work for the Ktunaxa Nation Council as an economic development director. "It was too good an opportunity to turn down," she recalls. "Promote a soccer team in a league whose future was questionable, or work for my First Nation to contribute to building my Nation's future for seven generations to come?" Edmonton didn't get a backward glance as Beverley hit the highway back to home territory.

Her new role was supervised by accomplished political leader Sophie Pierre, then chief of the St. Mary's Band[9] and chair of the Ktunaxa Nation. "I was so lucky to be offered the chance to work with Sophie. She is an amazing role model. She also believes in people, long before they know they should believe in themselves."

With the chief's encouragement, young Beverley leaped into the position with her sleeves rolled up, enthusiastically taking on challenging projects right from the get-go despite her lack of experience. "Sometimes not knowing what you're doing is a good thing!" she chuckles. "I was pretty new and keen. I just had the idea that if something was important to the Ktunaxa, we should be doing it, and we *could* do it—why not? My dream was that one day we and other First Nations would again be the leaders of the economy in their homelands." She adds: "Sometimes other people have to tell you that you can do it before you realize that you really can do it." Within a short time Beverley found herself working with teammates juggling a million-dollar pipeline right-of-way clearing project, and putting together the capital to invest in an ambitious hotel resort and golf course to be built on the grounds of a former Indian residential school on Ktunaxa land. "That was just the start of it," she says. "I learned so much in that job."

Beverley was the only Ktunaxa Nation member in the economic development team apart from her boss, Pierre. As operations manager, she went to many economic-related meetings that Pierre was too busy to attend. The chief knew that Beverley could do it—after all, she had been there herself as a young woman. "I would be sitting among people twice my age," Beverley marvels. "Often I would be the only woman there, and I was *always* the

9 See "Thoughts from Sophie Pierre," page 222.

only Aboriginal person in the room in those days. I felt the world weighing on my shoulders, that I bore a great sense of responsibility for future generations, and the fear of that tormented me. I needed to take that responsibility seriously," she says. "I just had to keep going and work hard and believe I could do it. Sometimes it was the belief from others around me that gave me the confidence I needed."

As much as anything, Beverley was in the right place at the right time. Of course, with her devotion to personal accountability, she thinks that everyone is always in the right place at the right time—"It's what you make of it." All the same, it *was* a good time to be in her economic development role for Ktunaxa. As the law increasingly favoured Aboriginal legal rights and title through the 1980s and 1990s, private companies and governments found they could no longer ignore Aboriginal peoples and became more and more receptive and eager to do business with First Nations. In her job, Beverley was exposed to politics and bureaucracy, learned the intricacies of both, and met frequently with company presidents, senior officials, politicians and future premiers of every stripe.

It was a priceless education in how the system works, something that staying in Edmonton could never have provided. "Sometimes you have to start over at home to make a better beginning," she says. "I'm glad I dreamed beyond the finish line, and had the courage to get in there and take that job, in a role I wasn't certain I could do. But I believed I could do it, and trusted that others knew I could. It was the best thing I could have done."

It was also challenging, of course. She had high expectations of herself: "I wanted to see things change for the better." She attributes the sense of responsibility in her makeup to her grandfather Toby Nicholas—at least in part. "In World War II, like many First Nations men, my grandfather enlisted to fight for a country that didn't even recognize him as a citizen, let alone as a person." He died in Sicily in 1943, and is buried there along with other Canadian soldiers. "I often wonder why he went, since he couldn't vote in Canada and had been treated so badly in this country. Why did he fight for Canada? Why were First Nations men and women the highest ratio per capita of *any* Canadian ethnic group who enlisted? Why would they defend a country, a world, that didn't recognize them as human beings?"

At first Beverley thought there must be a single answer to that question. "I'm ashamed that one of my initial thoughts was that perhaps he just wanted to get away from here to see the world, like any other adventurous young person." But as she reread the more than thirty letters her grandfather had sent home from the front, she gleaned a deeper purpose to his actions.

"There is seldom one answer to any question—I learned that in marketing," she says. "He wrote frequently in his letters that he just wanted to make this world a better place, and decided he needed to take responsibility for it." It's a message she has taken to heart as her own: "I think that's why I do what I do. Like my grandfather, I wanted to do something to help the Ktunaxa and other First Nations return to being leaders in their homelands, to make a better life for their people and others who have chosen to live in their territory."

After several years in her job, however, Beverley needed to find a way to move on to the next stage of her life. "It was inevitable that I would leave the tribal council at some point," she recalls. "I knew I would have to broaden my horizons eventually, and by 1994 I had to think about my future as the anniversary of my four-year commitment to my position at the KNC was coming up. I was twenty-nine years old—a single, professional female and First Nations person with big ideas, living in a place where I belonged but didn't belong at the same time. I knew though that no matter where I went in this world, I was always going to be welcome back home, and there was no better time in my life to take a leap of faith in myself."

In Cranbrook, she faced a constant barrage of stereotypical questions and comments for a young woman, let alone a First Nations woman: "Why don't you get married?" "You should be having children by now!" "Where's your boyfriend?" "What's wrong with you?" Leaving for the bigger city of Vancouver was not only appealing but made sense. "I spent a lot of time in the city anyway for work and on various committees and boards, so I had many contacts. I didn't actually intend to start my own business, but when a number of things I thought were supposed to happen didn't, starting a business was exactly what I ended up doing."

Beverley applied for a job in Vancouver. She was optimistic, but came in as second choice. "I wasn't sure what I was going to do when I didn't get the job. I had already started to leave Cranbrook in my mind, so I tried to think about where else I would want to work. I kept reminding myself everything happens for a reason, even if you don't understand why at the time. You have to trust and take a leap of faith."

She was cooling her heels in Vancouver trying to figure out what to do when a friend asked her why she didn't start her own business. She drove back to Cranbrook the next day, pondering the suggestion. "It's a long trip, and I had a lot of time to think about my future, and take inventory of my skills." It made a lot of sense, since she was already writing business plans and advising on operations for people of Ktunaxa; she knew she would be far more effective in providing business advice if she had experience running her own enterprise. After arriving home, she sat down and wrote her first business plan for herself.

She didn't know at first what fields she was going to focus on. "But I decided to go for it anyway. I'm a right- *and* left-brain thinker. Economic development, business, and marketing consulting all offer the opportunity to be both creative and logical. I've always liked drawing and writing, as well as accounting and problem solving, and marketing in particular offers a good balance of all those things." Beverley also realized that she had an inherent edge in a highly competitive field. "At the time, there really weren't any Aboriginal marketing consultants out there, and I hoped I could offer something that would be a bit different, especially to First Nations and governments working with First Nations."

Her theory was proven almost immediately. "When I told

Sophie I was leaving Ktunaxa, she said 'Good!' I was shocked and confused. She was happy I was leaving? Then she immediately said, 'We'll hire you.' It was a great way to start!" With her first contract securely in hand, Beverley packed her bags and moved to Vancouver a couple of months later. She started marketing her skills through a column in the First Nations newspaper *Kahtou*. Looking back, she says, "I knew I was doing what I was supposed to be doing. It felt right."

More than eighteen years later, with her businesses O'Neil Marketing & Consulting and Numa Communications Ltd., she is as busy, she says with satisfaction, as she wants to be. Among her other commitments, she has served on the boards of directors of Tourism British Columbia, Leadership Vancouver, Routes to Learning Canada, the Vancouver Aquarium, the BC Wine Institute, and the BC Energy Council. In addition to numerous First Nations clients, she has worked for the Yukon and Northwest Territory governments; the Canadian National Aboriginal Tourism Association; the Canadian Tourism Commission; Canadian Heritage; Agriculture and Agri-Food Canada; the Department of Foreign Affairs; and Indian and Northern Affairs Canada (now called Aboriginal Affairs and Northern Development Canada).

In 1997 she launched the Aboriginal Tourism Association of BC. In 2010, under contract for AtBC, she created the Aboriginal Cultural Tourism Authenticity Accreditation program, a certification program for First Nations tourism ventures that she says is now internationally regarded as a best practices leader in tourism certification. She led the development of the Aboriginal Cultural Tourism Blueprint Strategy in 2005, as well as projects associated with identifying Aboriginal opportunities and branding associated with the 2010 Winter Olympic Games in Vancouver.

Along the way, she has confirmed to herself many times over what the important things in life are: community, cultural values and contributing. All three continue to form the platform from which Beverley tackles new experiences, her responsibilities in life, and her relationships. "To me, community means you have to care about the people around you. It's one of the things I love about working in Aboriginal circles. People care about you and they care about each other. It's not just business. It's about people wanting to make life better, it's about relationships—not just for First Nations, but for whoever they are or whatever their background or wherever they are from."

In Canada, says Beverley, that's a labour of love for the most part. "It certainly isn't for the money. I think that many people don't understand that money is not the driving force for everyone. Success to me isn't measured by the size of a bank account. The people I admire don't flaunt success with the tangible things they've bought. The people I admire, and believe change the world for the better, are intelligent, caring, hard-working and dedicated people who could work anywhere but they choose to work to support First Nations. They are people who are really making a difference and leaving a legacy of a better world behind them."

At a cultural level, Beverley sees nothing but opportunity for First Nations people, especially in business—as long as they hold onto the fundamental principles and values of their culture. "I've travelled to Guyana twice, to do workshops on indigenous tourism principles and work with the Makushi people in the North Rupununi. In Surama village, where there is a sustainable eco-lodge that has received international accolades, I learned how the determination and values and sense of responsibility of a collective community can combine to supersede the expectations and offers of a corporation."

Beverley was concerned that the Makushi were at risk of losing the charm and authenticity of their cultural tourism experiences because they were being told by non-indigenous people to do things differently. "I learned that although we come from places that are thousands of miles apart, we share the same values and fears. At the same time I was reminded again by them that the key to success is being true to yourself and your identity. I had nothing to worry about, after all. These people are so well grounded in their culture and what that means in terms of the benefits for cultural tourism, economic development and governance, that I found I learned from them as much—if not more—than I think they learned from me."

She sees the same opportunities for success in Canada. "By 2015, one out of five people entering the workforce in Winnipeg will be a First Nations person, and in other parts of Canada our labour force presence and importance will only magnify. Our cultural values will be more and more influential in how business is done. We have to anticipate that. There are going to be many benefits for everyone as a result of that. Everyone will also gain when we see children growing up proud to be First Nations and getting out and succeeding in business and careers because of that pride and the cultural values they hold. Those kids are everyone's future."

As to Beverley's own professional future, the finish line remains far out of sight. Even if it was once visible, she's still looking past it and seeing nothing but opportunity and responsibility to do more. Maybe she'll slow down; she knows that when things are easy, it's a good time to regain energy to face whatever challenges lie ahead. On the personal front, every year she tries something new and different—perhaps a course in a fresh subject, or another writing project. Recently, she has been indulging a formerly suppressed passion to act. In 2011 she took a few comedy courses with the objective of becoming a stand-up comic. That in turn led to private acting lessons in late 2012.

Beverley starts laughing as she talks about it. "When I was a teenager everybody told me I was so serious," she says. "But I'm not. People tell me I'm always trying to crack jokes. In Edmonton, in 1988, I went to a comedy show and got called up on stage and the crowd loved my impromptu repartee with the comedian. I've always wanted to try something like this. I have become a stand-up comic, and I'm having a great time. It's another very creative outlet for me that I know you have to work hard at, and I do."

Her innate sense of responsibility is built into this aspect of her life as much as any other. "If you're going to do it, you have a responsibility to make people laugh, even though the textbooks

Nikki was Beverley's beloved companion for many years.
Courtesy Beverley O'Neil

say don't worry about the audience," she says firmly. "It's no different in that respect from the other work I do—it's about making people feel good, opening eyes, opening minds, opening hearts. For me, it's freeing, it's empowering, it's rewarding, and most of all," she repeats, "I feel like I'm doing what I'm supposed to do."

Her comic schtick is based on her life as a single professional woman. "I call the routine 'The quest of the alpha female in search of the new millennium man,'" she says with a sly smile. She is big on dating and relationship jokes, with the occasional "cougar" joke thrown in: "I was out on a date with a *much* younger guy. When I asked him what his hobbies are, he said: 'I like to collect antiques.'" Get it? Ouch. Actually, that's very funny, when you think about it. "I've been told my humour is very cranial. You do have to think about it! But so far, so good—the audiences seem to like it."

There's a tinge of wistfulness to the routine. "I still struggle sometimes with expectations and assumptions," she says. "I'm expected to be or do various things. I'm certainly not expected to be single and childless at my age. I get people telling me I'm living my life wrong, or making assumptions about my lifestyle, or that I'm unhappy or unfulfilled because I am single, when that's definitely not the case. We all make the life we choose." Hence the cougar jokes, which help to take the edge off those stereotypical ideas. "I'd rather be single and happy than in a relationship and with the wrong person." Laughter, as usual, is the best medicine.

Beverley will probably run quite a few more marathons before she's done. She has taken a creative writing course at Simon Fraser University, and is applying the skills she has learned to her two book projects. They follow themes from her childhood and her grandfather Toby's story, and explore the racism that her mother and grandmother each experienced as children and adults. She hopes to see her stories in print one day.

In the meantime, she says, she will keep on working on her own self-improvement, always looking for ways in which she can contribute and fulfill the responsibility to her people that she carries with her every day and the responsibility to what she feels she's supposed to do: with open mind, open eyes and open heart, always aiming well and truly past the finish line.

11: On the Battle Line

Maybe if we had always been able to control our own future the whole way along and make our own choices, there wouldn't be such a burden now of having to fight, of having to put ourselves on the battle line all the time. For our children, I hope it will be different. That's what I'm going to keep fighting for.

Merle Alexander, b. 1971
Kitasoo/Xai'xais First Nation, Klemtu/ North Vancouver
Aboriginal resource lawyer
Indigenous advocate within the United Nations
Alumnus (2009), *Business in Vancouver* Top Forty Under 40
Father, husband and travel enthusiast

"The work I do as an Aboriginal resource lawyer is interwoven into the fabric of everything I am as a person," Merle Alexander says. "My work, my beliefs, how I see myself as a member of society and my community, and my role in it as both a lawyer and the custodian of a hereditary title of the Raven clan, are all inseparable."

To an outsider it seems inevitable now that all those different threads would have become intrinsically interwoven in Merle's life. It may not have appeared that way at first, but the path to becoming a First Nations lawyer, living and breathing his work in defending First Nations' rights, is one he was probably born on.

His mother, Stella, who is of both Heiltsuk and Tsimshian heritage, grew up in a tiny Kitasoo/Xai'xais community on remote Swindle Island on British Columbia's north-central coast. By the

Merle Alexander
Courtesy Bull, Housser & Tupper LLP

time Merle was born in 1971, Stella and Merle's father were living in North Vancouver. Just eight months later, the family moved to Terrace, in northwestern British Columbia. At the time, Merle says, his mother had no desire to move her family back to Klemtu, the village of her childhood. "It's hard for kids to overcome the disadvantages of being in an isolated community, like limited access to good schools," Merle says. "She knew that because she had experienced it herself. She didn't want that for us."

Merle and his siblings visited Swindle Island every summer, all the same, and he has fond memories of fishing there with his grandfather. "Looking back now, I think that is what gave me such an innate connection to the place," he reflects. "I was very young but you unconsciously absorb what is happening around you and learn from it."

Growing up in a northern resource industry–based town like Terrace also gave him an education in First Nations concerns, one that his mother hadn't anticipated. "There's no doubt being raised there formed my original perspectives on relations in British Columbia between Aboriginal and non-Aboriginal people," Merle reflects. "Terrace was a pretty red-necked town in those days. That was at the height of the 'War in the Woods' too."

The infamous 1980s–'90s War in the Woods on the BC north and central coasts pitted logging companies, environmentalists, First Nations and the provincial government against each other as the various factions fought for control of the region's precious forestry resources and habitat. "There was a lot of conflict because everyone's income was based on use of all the natural resources in the area. The big companies were basically pillaging the territory and the First Nations were trying to oppose that and stop it, so it created this natural adversity between the First Nations and everyone else in the area who wanted the jobs and income from the exploitation of our resources."

As a young man, Merle wasn't particularly focused on those issues. In 1991, however, shortly after turning twenty, he started a political science degree at the University of Victoria on Vancouver

Island. There he really started to learn about the history of his people. He also made the connection between the negative impacts of colonization that were continuing to detract from the rights of First Nations and what he had witnessed for himself growing up in Terrace.

It was a complete eye-opener for the impressionable young man, who was actively looking for a cause to take on. "I was a really feisty twenty-year-old," he says. "I'd had a life-changing and inspirational turning point in my life that year: I'd broken my neck in a cycling accident and was in traction for four months. It was a real wake-up call about my own mortality, at a very early age. It also made me believe that there was a meaning for my life, that the Creator gave me this opportunity. So when I went to university and was learning the history of my people, and really understanding for the first time what their struggle represented, it made me want to fight. I became very politically involved, joining the Young New Democrats and going onto their executive. That's also when I decided to go to law school. Where else better to go, to start fighting the battle?"

After completing his BA in political science, Merle spent a year in an Aboriginal consulting firm working with First Nations on treaty negotiations and the protection of cultural heritage sites. He also undertook research for First Nations clients involved in the federal government's specific claims process, a forum for negotiations to resolve outstanding grievances of First Nations under their historic treaties—breaches by the government of its obligations under such treaties, for example, or historical removal of portions of reserve land without the consent of the affected First Nation.

That experience left Merle more determined than ever to pursue law, and in 1995 he applied for and was accepted to the University of Victoria law co-op program. "The law co-op provided me with some tremendous opportunities, including working on a fast-paced treaty negotiation table for one summer. I was also involved with doing legal research, and was able to watch the advocacy work related to the landmark *Delgamuukw* Aboriginal title case."

The 1997 Supreme Court of Canada decision in *Delgamuukw v. British Columbia* confirmed the existence of Aboriginal title to land and water in the province, requiring the federal and provincial governments to consult First Nations on decisions affecting such title. For First Nations in British Columbia, the case signalled a fundamental shift in their favour in the balance of power between them and governments; it was a tremendously exciting moment for a young Aboriginal law student to witness. The court also urged First Nations and governments to negotiate mutually satisfactory agreements to reconcile Aboriginal title and Crown jurisdiction, famously stating: "Let us face it: we are all here to stay."

In 1999, Merle transferred to the University of Toronto to complete the last semester of his law degree. "I was following my heart at the time, or I would never have gone there," he recalls. "What a shock Toronto was! It was the biggest city I had ever been to, and I'd never experienced anything like it." After completing his degree, Merle stayed in the city. He landed a job at a Bay Street law firm where he had served a co-op term. "It was overwhelming at first. I didn't know anyone in Toronto, and I didn't have a chance to get to know anyone because of the insane lifestyle I was living,

Merle received his law degree in 1999 from the University of Victoria.
Courtesy Merle Alexander

working day and night. I just went back and forth from my apartment to the office and lived on food from the food courts in the concourse below Bay Street. It was crazy!"

Nonetheless, his time in the big city law firm also proved to be invaluable experience for a young lawyer with big dreams of heading back home one day to defend the rights of his people. "The law firm I was working for was representing the Innu Nation and other First Nations clients in self-government negotiations in Labrador, and in discussions on the impact of the Upper Churchill Falls hydroelectricity project and the Voisey Bay nickel mine." The stories Merle heard in the course of his work about the destruction of traditional lifestyles also cemented his determination to fight for First Nations. "It was brutal," he says sombrely. "We heard about children dying of gas inhalation, about strings of suicides in small communities. We were told about a house that blew up, killing seventeen kids. That kind of thing just seemed to be endless."

While undertaking research to support the Innu claims, Merle also unwittingly set off on a path that would lead to an unexpected new role. "I had been working on their intellectual property rights—their rights to protection and use of their cultural knowledge—and inclusion of those rights in their treaty. As part of that work, I was sent to a meeting in Ottawa that no one else wanted to go to. I was the most junior member of the team, so I drew the short straw. But I didn't mind, it sounded really interesting. I also had never been that far east in Canada, so I wanted to go."

The meeting was with a couple of United Nations groups looking at the importance of using Aboriginal traditional knowledge to help protect biodiversity. As the UN representatives and indigenous advocates began to speak, Merle was spellbound. He was completely captivated by the idea that one of the world's most important international bodies was so profoundly interested in protecting cultural rights so as to help protect biodiversity.

"It made me realize for the first time how big the issue was. Until then I had just been focused on Canada. Now I understood that it was actually a global issue. I realized that First Nations in Canada

Merle listening intently at one of the many United Nations committee meetings he attended in his twelve-year role as an indigenous advocate.
Courtesy Merle Alexander

shared the same struggles to protect their rights and to have their cultural knowledge respected in protecting biodiversity as other indigenous people all over the world." Merle was fascinated by the potential to harness collective global indigenous power to win that fight in particular and the battle to protect indigenous rights in general. "I decided on the spot to get myself involved in the work that the United Nations was doing."

The meeting with the UN groups took place early in 1998, and Merle didn't waste a moment to get more deeply involved. For the next twelve years, he devoted several months a year to acting as a United Nations indigenous legal advocate, working on various UN committees in Geneva alongside other indigenous advocates from around the world, and travelling across the globe to participate in meetings on every continent except Antarctica.

While he was in the role he also witnessed Canada's adoption of the draft UN Declaration on the Rights of Indigenous Peoples, a political affirmation of the moral and political obligations of states to honour those rights. The Canadian government had vigorously resisted adopting the draft declaration for more than a decade, but in 2010 it finally capitulated. "Better late than never," Merle says wryly. "It's a very powerful moral commitment and it's significant to have it in place here now. In the UN context, it immediately became a very influential vehicle that the indigenous advocates could refer to in their specific areas of work. It is without question being used as a stepping stone to implement real, incremental and meaningful change."

It was a whirlwind and exciting period of his life, but he never lost sight of the importance of the primary objective of building international consensus on protection of indigenous rights. "I was very involved with the development of the Nagoya Protocol [on Access to Genetic Resources and Associated Traditional Knowledge and the Fair and Equitable Sharing of Benefits Arising from their Utilization]." The protocol was adopted in April 2010. "As far as I know, it remains one of the only forums in the United Nations where indigenous people had real negotiations authority. After all that time, the indigenous advocates had become very experienced and sophisticated in their approach. We had built enough credibility in our approach and in our positions to have earned that rightful place at the negotiations table."

That represented significant progress in favour of indigenous groups from the time when Merle had first started working with the UN. "It was pretty amazing to witness that evolution from the beginning, when the advocates had to beg at the door to get Canada and other countries to bring basic indigenous issues to the table. Over time, as indigenous peoples became an accepted and legitimate voting bloc, we also became a negotiating party that countries were coming to, to ask us for our support. I chaired a couple of the UN committee meetings, and it was a complete role reversal from the old days—now the Canadian delegation had to ask me for permission to speak rather than the other way round. That was a very powerful and exciting change."

Certain that things would only continue to improve in that regard, Merle finally put an end to his United Nations work in late

2010. His decision was driven in part by his desire to focus on his legal work back home. He was also keen, following his marriage that year to First Nations lawyer Tamara Olding, to put an end to his onerous travel schedule.

He felt immensely satisfied with the progress that had been made during his tenure, and hung up his UN hat with little regret, countless good memories, and dozens of lifelong friendships forged in the trenches of international indigenous rights protection. "There's this remarkable bond between all the indigenous people involved in that work," he says with deep pleasure in his voice. "Even more importantly, there's a cultural global connection at a tribal level that is very empowering and important in terms of international indigenous influence over states."

Although he was leaving his international work in good hands, Merle wasn't about to rest on his laurels. There were still plenty of battles to fight back home in Canada, despite a positive trend in relationship-building among First Nations, governments and industry that had resulted from the *Delgamuukw* decision as well as several subsequent Supreme Court of Canada cases that had also strongly supported Aboriginal rights.

The legal decisions had placed an onus on governments and industry to consult First Nations before undertaking business activities affecting the land and resources in their territories, and to not only accommodate their interests but to ensure environmental protection of those resources. "It was a very good place for people to start working together instead of fighting all the time," Merle recalls. "First Nations finally started to be heard about protection of the environment and their traditional lands. They also started to see some real benefits from the appropriate use of their resources, with a share of profits going to them instead of into the pockets of private industry. Governments and industry learned that working alongside First Nations instead of trying to go over their heads worked much more efficiently, with better results all round."

But by 2008 the global economy had begun to falter. "Business started getting nervous and more protective of its bottom line,"

Merle says. "Companies were just trying to survive and the First Nations component of their business came to be seen as more of a liability than an asset. As a result, things have become much more adversarial again now, unfortunately. Companies have pulled back on how much they invest in liaison with First Nations in the areas where they are doing business, and they are trying to really cut down on what they bring to the table in negotiating agreements with First Nations. They still want us to support their projects, but they don't want to pay for it."

What Merle describes as an emasculation of environmental laws by a "rapacious and highly adversarial" federal government in 2012 didn't help. First Nations faced a tougher fight than ever if they opposed environmentally degrading industrial projects, and neither the federal nor provincial governments of the day showed any great interest in meaningful consultation with First Nations, despite their legal obligations. By the beginning of 2013 it seemed inevitable that another slew of Aboriginal rights cases would be heading for the courts.

While he wishes it didn't have to be that way, Merle also sees a silver lining: "Backward-minded governments and businesses actually create very good Aboriginal rights case law, because the worse they get at fulfilling their constitutional obligations to Aboriginal people, the more case law they unintentionally generate that will support our rights, and which therefore can be used positively to our advantage." It's a shame it has to come to that. "Yes, it certainly is. You'd think the concept of working together instead of fighting all the time would be obvious. Who doesn't want to get on with their neighbours?" he asks, echoing the views of Osoyoos Indian Band Chief Clarence Louie.[10] "Who doesn't enjoy having a good relationship?"

But in the absence of such sensible behaviour, from governments in particular, Merle points out that there are also some other unexpected consequential benefits emerging for First Nations—and for Canadian society generally. "For the first time,

10 See "Thoughts from Clarence Louie," page 103.

in a really significant way, First Nations aren't alone on the battle line against governments anymore. I think the average Canadian also feels that the government is working against their rights, and are seeing some real interests in common with Aboriginal Canadians in a way that we've never seen before. More and more, non-Aboriginal people are seeing what has been happening, seeing how First Nations people resist, and joining in the groundswell of opposition against the tyranny."

Merle points to the Idle No More movement as an example. "They came out swinging, saying 'enough is enough' to the government, and look at how many non-Aboriginal people joined the movement worldwide within the space of just a few days. Everyone was ready for something like this. That's really fantastic. It's something that has real potential to unite the citizens of this country, regardless of their cultural heritage, for the first time in a very long time."

For an indigenous rights activist, it has been enormously exciting to see such change unfold in his own country and his own province. Perhaps the most exhilarating development of all has been the creation of a new stable of young, politically savvy future leaders who are actively engaged in their communities. "People didn't see it, but there were Idle No More flash mobs everywhere in all these little communities on the coast. Even little Klemtu had one. There has been a real harnessing of the feelings of disenfranchisement, and instead of feeling powerless about it, turning those feelings around into a really significant sense of power and influence by taking these actions to protest against the government."

The timing may just happen to have been right, Merle believes. "The sheer speed at which the Idle No More movement took off in the space of just a few weeks was extraordinary. The fact that young Aboriginal people actually felt like their voices were being heard in Canadian society gave them a sense of connection for the first time to that society. I think that's just going to get stronger and stronger, with First Nations people getting out voting in greater numbers than ever before, maybe even running for elected office in the provincial or federal governments and trying to initiate change at those levels."

Merle is inspired by that possibility, but whether he will personally get involved in politics is undecided. His own family has a long and proud political history. He inherited his chief's name from his grandmother, whose name meant "a woman of high regard." His grandfather was a former chief, and worked as a councillor for twenty-two years. After the kids had grown up, his mother went back to university, obtained a degree and finally returned to Klemtu for good, eventually getting herself elected to Kitasoo/ Xai'xais Council.

Merle does envision some form of future role, political or otherwise, in Klemtu. "You never lose that tie to your territory," he says. "There's an undeniable closeness to the land, even if you haven't had the chance to grow up there." Right now, however, he and Tamara are a typical young professional couple enjoying building their careers and their busy lives in the big city. For a man who is equally comfortable in a boardroom or around a campfire,

Merle dancing with his mother, Stella, at his wedding.
Courtesy Lucida Photography, Melia Sorenson photo

Vancouver offers both scenarios. "I love the outdoors, and here I do lots of hiking, I play beach volleyball, I go snowshoeing in the winter. Tamara is helping me get the work/life balance a bit better in hand after all the intensity of the United Nations work. We really enjoy all the cultural activities the city offers. I really like foreign cinema, so we go to see foreign films whenever we can. I'm finally taking winter holidays in the sunshine to just relax and have fun. It's pretty nice, I must say."

Professionally, his legal work on behalf of Aboriginal people remains his priority for the present. The battle lines are still drawn, and he feels a great responsibility to keep fighting. "I would work hard at anything and I think I would succeed at whatever I set out to do, but right now, this is it. Working on Aboriginal rights is a huge gravitational pull for First Nations people who want to make a difference."

That comes with a lot of pressure. "At times it feels as much a burden as a privilege," Merle admits. "In law school, I felt real pressure to succeed because I kept thinking I would be letting my First

Merle and Tamara Olding, also an Aboriginal lawyer, on their wedding day in 2010.
Courtesy Lucida Photography, Melia Sorenson photo

Nation down if I failed. The average Canadian law student probably doesn't sit in class thinking about whether he's going to let Canada down, but the reality is that is what a lot of First Nations students have to deal with. They feel responsible to live up to the standards of their culture and to succeed for the sake of their community and their nationhood. It's part of the legacy we inherited from the fact that First Nations are still having to fight for our rights—it almost channels you as a student into this line of work."

Merle hopes that one day in the not-too-distant future Aboriginal kids, like any other Canadian kids, will feel free to study whatever they want, without that kind of pressure on them. "I would like to think they could study entertainment law, or criminal law—whatever interested them—and not feel like they need to study Aboriginal rights law in order to help defend those rights. Maybe they want to study art. Maybe they will be the next Monet. They will be able to choose whatever they want to study—whatever influences, cultural or otherwise, are important to them."

He doesn't know how much has to change for that to happen. "Certainly, the next generation would ideally be free of having to fight for our rights. Those rights would be protected and implemented as a matter of course, and our people would be able to simply participate in life in British Columbia in whatever way they choose. I think one thing that would stem from that, but also support it, is a sense of pride in our heritage beginning right from earliest childhood." Now, Merle says, "it's much more common for Aboriginal people to look for lots of different ways to be proud of our heritage, through our language and our traditions and our cultural knowledge."

"Maybe if we had always been able to do that, if we had been able to control our own future the whole way along and make our own choices, there wouldn't be such a burden now of having to fight, of having to put ourselves on the battle line all the time. For our children, I hope it will be different. If I have to fight, that's what I'm going to keep fighting for."

Thoughts from Shawn A-in-chut Atleo

b. 1967

National Chief, Assembly of First Nations

(interviewed in 2004)

When you've had to sit in the Supreme Court of Canada in Ottawa and hear the federal and provincial governments deny we even exist as a people, it makes it pretty hard to even feel part of this country.

We still have to fight to be respected as indigenous peoples in this country. The entire mindset of colonialism—treating us as wards of the state under the Indian Act, residential schools, banning our culture—has been to make us feel less than human. I am an Ahousaht hereditary chief. That's a role I was born into, and one dictated by Ahousaht law. Ahousaht law existed before British Columbia or Canada did. That governance responsibility is unchangeable. Not to live by that law, not to govern ourselves that way, would be like trying to live without water or oxygen. That, you can't negotiate. You just have to do it.

Reconciliation is essential for me, for Ahousaht and for all indigenous Nations to feel connected and part of what is now called Canada. It is through recognition and implementation of partnership that we can all embrace our respectful roles, identities and responsibilities.

Photo courtesy Assembly of First Nations

12: A Matter of Choice

I had to own my own situation. If I wanted something better for myself, I had to choose to overcome the obstacles that faced me. Everyone faces challenges in life. My choices were to be a victim of those challenges, or to feel them, experience them, learn from them, and then make a conscious effort to create a new future and move into it.

Trudy Lynn Warner, b. 1975
Huu-ay-aht First Nations, Port Alberni
MA in leadership, Royal Roads University
Former Huu-ay-aht member of Maa-nulth treaty team
Communicator and certified coach
Insightful mom

The weather on July 28, 2007, wasn't unusual for a summer day on the west coast of Vancouver Island. Tendrils of fog hung from the dripping branches of dark green spruce, undisturbed by even the whisper of an offshore breeze. A cold drizzle scribbled abstract patterns on the opaque grey surf sloshing gently on Brady's Beach, near Bamfield. The regular contingent of surfers was nowhere to be seen. Local fishermen huddled on their boats in wool sweaters and heavy raingear, resigned to the typically dreary conditions. But that particular Saturday was anything but ordinary for the Huu-ay-aht people of British Columbia's West Coast.

Among them was a young woman named Trudy Lynn Warner.

Trudy Warner
Courtesy Trudy Warner

Trudy, who had spent the past twelve years of her life working for her First Nation toward the goal of a treaty, cast her vote that day in favour of a proposed agreement that had been worked out with the governments of Canada and British Columbia. She was not alone: an overwhelming majority of her fellow Huu-ay-aht citizens wholeheartedly endorsed the signing of a treaty on that extraordinary and life-changing summer's day.[11]

For Trudy, her vote was a choice to support her First Nation— not only to conclude a treaty and achieve the return of formally recognized self-government under Canadian law, but to overcome the barriers of Canada's *Indian Act*, and a past of colonial repression that encompassed the residential-school system, exclusion from basic citizenship and human rights, and the abrogation of fundamental legal rights. "It was without question a matter of choice," she says. "We wanted something better for ourselves. But we had to consciously choose to get it. No one else could do it for us."

For the Huu-ay-aht people, saying yes to a treaty was synonymous with choosing freedom: an end to life under the tyrannical regime of the *Indian Act*.[12] Trudy regards it as a brave choice as well. "We had to have unwavering focus and strength," she says emphatically. "My First Nation faced huge obstacles, but chose to overcome them despite how hard that was to do, despite having to overcome 150 years of suffering."

Trudy believes that part of that strength came from drawing on the Huu-ay-aht ancestors: "When I look back at that part of our history, I know we have been and continue to be guided on our path by our ancestors." She also believes things will only get better from here. "I think that we will only continue to get stronger once we are able to maximize the benefits of this treaty, and once we have fully healed from the past. There'll be no stopping us!"

Trudy smiles and falls silent, absent-mindedly stirring her hot water with lemon. There is nothing about the demeanour of this slim, relaxed and immaculately dressed young woman, trading

11 See "A Short History of the Maa-nulth Treaty," page 170.
12 See "Born to Be Free," page 174.

friendly greetings with other restaurant patrons in a cozy Port Alberni café, that hints at the power of her determination and courage, or the years of exhausting effort and the emotional toll she and her fellow Huu-ay-aht treaty team members endured to achieve their dream. Nothing gives away the hard reality that implementing the dream also continues to exact a demanding price.

Five years after the Huu-ay-aht vote took place Trudy was still working as a consultant to her First Nation, assisting with the transition to a post-treaty world. "The work required to implement the changes and to implement a new way of doing things in the post-treaty world has been tremendous," she observes. "It's been absolutely worthwhile, but incredibly demanding." As she had for the previous few years, Trudy contributed what she could on the communications end: listening to Huu-ay-aht citizens, talking to them and to the decision makers and leaders, and offering them objective advice and suggestions for solutions.

It was a role the 2011 graduate of Royal Roads University's Master of Arts in Leadership program had played for a long time, and one that came naturally. "I felt that I had a magic chair in my office," she jokes. "People would come in and shut the door, sit, and share all their challenges with me. It happened a lot," she continues, serious once more. Trudy adds: "I hope that people think I'm a good listener, and empathetic. It was natural to listen and ask questions, and to make suggestions and tell them what I saw and felt as an observer that they could do to deal with those challenges."

A professional career in communications seemed like a logical choice as a next step. Typically, the determined young woman didn't let the fact that she only had a high school diploma stand in the way of applying for the master's program at Royal Roads. With glowing references behind her and a track record of doing what she set out to do, in 2009 the university welcomed her with open arms. Two years later, she walked out again with her MA. In November 2012 she augmented it with a graduate certificate in executive coaching and launched her own coaching and leadership consultancy business in Port Alberni.

A professional career of any kind wasn't on Trudy's mind when she first started working for the Huu-ay-aht treaty team at the age of twenty. "Oh no," she smiles, "I was far more interested in my social life then to have paid close attention to treaty issues or band politics or the challenges the community was facing." The young woman simply wanted a better job, and the new treaty office in Port Alberni was advertising for a cultural inventory research assistant. She applied and landed the position, adding reception and administrative duties to her job description as time went on. "That was really the start of it all," she recalls. "That's when my eyes started to open up."

It was also a new world for someone who had spent more than half of her short life growing up on the remote Grappler Creek reserve on Barkley Sound, accessible only by boat. There was no electricity on that particular reserve, and only four houses. "For most of my childhood, there were only ever ten or fifteen people around Grappler Creek. I had cousins and one friend, Sarie, to play with outside school hours. Every morning, rain or shine, Sarie's dad would take us to elementary school in Bamfield by speedboat." Trudy loved it: she couldn't have imagined a better childhood, and she adored both Grappler Creek and the relatively bright lights of Bamfield.

The young girl lived with her mother and grandfather. Her father, who was not First Nations, was never a part of her life except in one respect: hair and skin that were lighter than those of her cousins and Huu-ay-aht friends. "That was very difficult for me," reflects Trudy. "As a child, your family represents everything to you—safety, security, a sense of identity. I desperately wanted to look just like the rest of the family. In my head and heart I was 100 percent First Nations just like them, but my skin contradicted that notion."

The childhood angst about her appearance eventually disappeared, diminished by the normal trials and tribulations suffered by all teenagers as she grew older. Far more traumatic was the sudden death of her mother when Trudy was only eleven. On top of the grievous loss, Trudy now faced the end of her idyllic existence at Grappler Creek. "It was impossible to stay there with just my elderly grandfather. The decision was made that I had to move to Port Alberni to live with my aunt and uncle."

The little girl felt as if she had been caught up in a whirlwind. "The transition was really scary for me. If I could have stayed in Bamfield for the rest of my life, I would have without hesitation. I loved Bamfield so much, and Port Alberni was nothing short of intensely intimidating for an eleven-year-old who had led a pretty sheltered life. It was huge and foreign and lonely. I was right out of my comfort zone."

For the heartbroken child, it was also hard to keep up in school. Trudy went from an A student to a C+ student in Port Alberni, a shock to someone who was used to doing well at everything she tried. "On reflection, when I look back to my childhood, I can see the downward spiral I got caught up in after I lost my mom. I fell behind with everything. I was always playing catch-up, and really, I was just going through the motions most of the time. But you just keep going," she recalls of that time. "Even when you're a kid, life goes on. I didn't spend a lot of time thinking about it all back then."

Although she didn't realize it at the time, she experienced what would prove to be a pivotal life change when a friend's parents took her in at the age of sixteen, after her home life had become increasingly difficult in the wake of her uncle and aunt's divorce. "Everyone in the whole Spence family was wonderful to me," Trudy says. "They taught me so much as well as looking after me. For the first time, I was able to see the potential for life to be different.

"I pictured something different for myself too, but of course I didn't really know what back then. But I could see how hard these people worked, and how they had got themselves a nice home and nice things by working for them. They were happy in what they were doing and they were happy to share that with me. I was so fortunate." It was an enormously influential time in her life.

"I think that's when the cornerstones of learning to make good choices were put in place for me for the first time, even if I could not have articulated it that way back then."

All the same, after her high school graduation, Trudy continued to drift along for the next few years working low-wage jobs waitressing and in the local fish plant. When the treaty office job finally came up, however, the timing was perfect. "I realized that now I was twenty years old I couldn't use the excuse of losing my mom to act like a victim anymore. I had to own my own situation," she says. "If I wanted something better for myself, I had to choose to overcome the obstacles that faced me. Everyone faces challenges in life. My choices were to be a victim of it, or feel it, experience it, learn from it and then make a conscious effort to create a new future and move into it. Choosing to take the treaty office job was the first step in having the courage to expose myself to new opportunities and learning to make better choices for myself."

There was no looking back. Trudy quickly took on more responsibilities, moving up through the ranks of administrative assistant to become a full member of the Huu-ay-aht treaty team. "At that time, while of course I was aware of the issues facing the First Nation, I still wasn't paying that much attention to them. But then my team asked me to work on a consultation project related to creating the Huu-ay-aht constitution," she remembers.

The new Huu-ay-aht constitution would be a document setting out a framework for the post-treaty First Nation government and a process for making their own laws, as well as a system of financial administration and matters such as conflict-of-interest rules. To come into effect, it would have to be approved by the members of the Nation.

"So for about eight months I travelled to all our communities, and to many other places where community members were living, to talk to them about the new constitution, explain what it was and how it would work, and ask them what they thought should be in it." That experience, says Trudy, helped her grow in a big way. "At the beginning, I didn't clearly understand exactly what a constitution was. By doing that work, I learned so much about the treaty process, about things like the constitution, and the important issues for our communities and the people of our Nation."

Still only in her early twenties, Trudy also started to learn she had an innate capacity to analyze the issues and to communicate her thoughts to her team leaders in a way that would end up making an enormous difference to the work at hand. "She was a major force in our progress," reflects former Huu-ay-aht chief councillor Robert Dennis, who says that Trudy earned the respect of many of her peers on her own merits. "She used her communications skills to achieve this and in our culture, to earn the respect of your people is a great honour," Dennis emphasizes.

"I had a great relationship with our chief councillor," Trudy confirms. The relationship meant a great deal to a young woman who had never had a father in her life. "He told me how proud he was of me, like a father would be of a daughter." That gave her the confidence to be blunt with her leaders about needing to tackle the hard issues the community was raising. "I was very junior in the organization, but I always had to be upfront with the chief councillor, even if the information I was giving him was sometimes hard to share, and to give him my honest opinion. There were times after those kinds of conversations when I would be quite shocked at myself for telling him what I thought he should do about these things. But I had to. It felt like the right thing to do. Sometimes it was what the people had asked me to do for them. I know he wanted that too."

Trudy says that, looking back, she is immensely grateful for the unique opportunity she had to work with the leaders of her First Nation, people she credits as being of the highest calibre of intellect and integrity. "I was exposed to smart, humble, great people who were natural teachers. I was so fortunate to have that experience. It's been fundamental to who I have become as a person. I learned that your desire for something has to be stronger than your fear of what may hold you back in getting it. We had to have a strong desire to get to where we wanted to be. We still do."

Left: Trudy with her son, Jaden. *Courtesy Trudy Warner*

Right: Trudy is teaching Jaden about the importance of making good choices in life.
Roberto Nichele photo

That's something she also has to have in her personal life. Trudy became a single mother at the age of twenty-nine. After her own childhood experiences, she wanted her son, Jaden, to have everything she did not. So she set her own goals, and met them without relying on anyone else for help. Trudy now owns a modest home in a pleasant suburb of Port Alberni. She drives a comfortable, safe, late-model car. She practises traditional spiritual healing methods, firmly believes in feng shui, and makes sure she looks after her own health and well-being so she is in a good position to look after her family and the people she works with.

She calls Jaden an "old soul," and watches with wonder and joy in her heart as he grows up. He is in good hands: she has already taught him about making choices and putting the necessary effort and commitment into getting what he wants. She realizes too that she alone cannot give him all he needs, which is "very hard for me to accept, but it's a fact. As he gets older he is going to need more from other people and to hear, see and experience different things. I know other people made a huge difference to my life. They will to his too. Life would be very limited if we didn't get that exposure to other possibilities."

Trudy is also enjoying putting into practice what she learned in gaining her master's degree. "I can't believe how much I learned," she reflects. "The program content was enormous. I kept thinking, how is it possible to absorb and retain all of this information? But I had psyched myself up for it, and it was hugely rewarding." After her experiences in helping the leaders of her treaty team, Trudy took to the coaching component of her program like the proverbial duck to water.

"It was one of the most useful practical components of the whole experience," she says. "The thing with coaching is that you don't need to be an expert on the subject matter you are dealing with, you just need to know what questions to ask. It's all about helping people discover new ways of thinking and launching toward creating their success instead of being stuck in one place. Before coaching, I also thought that I had to solve their problems, but I learned that isn't my responsibility. It's about supporting *them* to achieve their goals, big or small."

Stepping back from the burden of having to solve everyone else's problems has been a huge relief. "I love the role of being a helper. It's the right role for me. It's so much easier now!" Because Trudy is a good listener and empathetic, coaching was a natural fit: "I can see the forest instead of the trees and show them the way." But life is all about choices, Trudy emphasizes, and it's up to each individual to take responsibility to get what he or she wants out of life. "We can't always control what happens to us in life, but we can control how we respond to what happens. From my perspective, it's always a matter of choice."

It feels like a very long time since that chilly fog-bound day in 2007 when Trudy and her First Nation made the choice to enter into a treaty with British Columbia and Canada. But it still has the firm feel of the right choice. She is looking ahead already, planning for how to assess progress and measure success. Failure is clearly not an option. "You must have to have something to strive for in life," she muses. "You can't ever stop learning and working for something better. Otherwise you're not really living."

She continues to spend time in Port Alberni and Bamfield, and still assists Huu-ay-aht with treaty implementation and communications work, helping her Nation to strengthen and nurture its relationships within its own organization and community, and with its treaty partners. "Through the years of work and learning I've realized how important relationships are in First Nations culture, at every level—individual, organizational, and community-to-community relationships," Trudy says. "This treaty is intended to support a positive new relationship. But it takes time to build a relationship. The process of building trust and mutual respect takes great care.

"It's all about intention," she concludes. Trudy smiles, gazing at the grey skies above Alberni Inlet. "It's all about making the right choices."

A Short History of the Maa-nulth Treaty

In 2007 the people of the Huu-ay-aht, Ka:'yu:'k't'h'/ Che:k'tles7et'h, Toquaht Nation, Uchucklesaht Tribe and Ucluelet First Nation—collectively known as the Maa-nulth First Nations—gathered to vote on one of the most important issues they would ever deal with in their lives: a proposed umbrella treaty agreement between each of their Nations and the governments of Canada and British Columbia, to be known—if approved—as the Maa-nulth treaty.

In British Columbia, only fourteen treaties had been concluded before Confederation in 1871, all on Vancouver Island (Treaty 8, which spills over from Alberta into the northeast of the province, was negotiated in 1899). The Nisga'a First Nation, located in the

Members of the five Maa-nulth Nations approach the Legislature to witness the historic ratification of their treaty by the BC government in 2007. Their treaty became a reality on April 1, 2011. © 2013, Province of British Columbia

remote Nass Valley on the north coast of British Columbia, concluded a treaty in 2000. It was the first such treaty in the province since Confederation.

Several explanations are possible for the lack of treaty-making in British Columbia compared to the rest of Canada, which is blanketed by historic treaty agreements. One explanation is that the British government ran out of money for further purchases after Governor James Douglas signed his last treaty in 1854. Another is that it simply wasn't thought necessary. Enough land been purchased on Vancouver Island for settlement, and it was quickly realized that Indian reserves could be created without treaties and that no more time had to be wasted in negotiations.

After Confederation, the new provincial government also had jurisdiction over almost all of the land in British Columbia, but it was an express term of Confederation that the federal government would continue to take responsibility for Indians, and therefore for Indian lands. The province was not about to give up any of its newly acquired Crown lands to the federal government in order to create more Indian reserves.

In the meantime, government-sanctioned discrimination and repressive measures continued for decades. Indians registered under the *Indian Act,* first passed in 1876, were treated like wards of the state rather than independent adults. They were prohibited from pre-empting land or voting in either provincial or federal elections. They were forbidden to fish commercially, practise traditions such as potlatch, or drink in public bars. Until 1951, it was illegal for Indians to hire lawyers to pursue land claims. Their children were sent to residential schools. There was little they could do to fight back.

The *Indian Act* does provide what might seem to outsiders like perks, such as the tax exemption on reserves and annual funding from what used to be called Indian and Northern Affairs Canada (INAC) but which has since been changed to Aboriginal and Northern Affairs Canada (although INAC, DIA and Indian Affairs remain the more common ways of referring to the department).

Indian band governments struggle, though, to meet community needs on INAC money alone. Because Indian reserves are owned by the federal government rather than the bands, it is difficult for band governments to attract investment partners for economic development projects that could supplement their meagre revenues. The federal government also holds band cash in trust under the *Indian Act,* and chiefs and councils must ask the minister of Aboriginal and Northern Affairs for permission to spend any of it.

The act also doesn't recognize laws that First Nations had in place to govern their society before European contact. The Maanulth peoples have always been governed by Ta'yii Ha'with, hereditary chiefs who are responsible for the well-being of their people and stewardship of the traditional territory. Elected *Indian Act* governments are not traditional, and by comparison, have severely limited bylaw-making powers weighed down by unwieldy and bureaucratic federal chains.

During one winter's storms, for example, a few years before the Maa-nulth treaty came into effect, hundreds of trees blew down at the Pachena Bay campground, located on a Huu-ay-aht reserve near Bamfield. Before the Huu-ay-aht chief and council could arrange to remove the logs and sell them, they had to seek Ottawa's permission. That took five months to obtain—a typical length of time. The money then went into an INAC trust account instead of band coffers.

"We had to make a proposal to the minister about how we would like to use the money, and he decided whether we would spend it in an appropriate manner," Huu-ay-aht Councillor Tom Mexsis Happynook says. "This was our life for 130 years." It is easy to understand why, when the modern treaty process in British Columbia was initiated in 1993, Tom's community and many others leaped on the opportunity to change their lives. The members of the Maa-nulth First Nations approved their deal nearly fifteen years later, in 2007, and the treaty came into effect on April 1, 2011.

For the Maa-nulth peoples, the long wait was worth it. Their agreement represents recognition and protection of their traditional rights, a prosperous and healthy future for their communities, and, at long last, liberation from the antiquated constraints of the *Indian Act.*[13]

---

13 See "What's in the Tsawwassen Treaty," page 118, for a description of the content of a similar agreement.

13: Born to Be Free

We shocked everyone when we told the government we were ready for a treaty. We had to shrug off the naysayers and take the risk. But we are ready, and I'd rather be free.

Evan Touchie, b. 1974 – d. 2007
Yuułuʔiłʔatḥ/Ucluelet First Nation
Band councillor
Husband and dad
Passionate supporter of the Maa-nulth treaty
Believer in freedom

Evan Touchie, surfer, basketball player, runner, weightlifter, died of a heart attack in 2007, at the age of thirty-three. A few weeks later his grieving widow, Melody, wrote on Touchie's memorial Facebook page: "I was becoming very concerned about Evan's health, especially after watching this episode on *Oprah*. Dr. Oz was talking about heart attacks and food. How it doesn't matter if you are young—that if you are not eating well, you can have a heart attack." Evan, highly athletic and apparently very fit, had thought he was invincible and eaten unhealthy food with gusto all his life. "He thought because he was so fit, that nothing like that could happen to him," Melody wrote. "Sadly, that wasn't the case."

Evan's unexpected loss shocked the Ucluelet community to its core. That wasn't simply because he was a young, beautiful man, an adoring father to his young children and a devoted husband. The young people of Ucluelet looked up to him as a role model of

Evan Touchie
Jonathan Clark/Maa-nulth Treaty Society

someone who had once been going down the wrong track but had turned in the right direction before it was too late.

Sober for the two years before his death, Evan became an active member of his community over that period of time, working hard on behalf of the Yuułuʔiłʔatḥ (Ucluelet) First Nation as a recently elected band councillor and an advocate for the Maa-nulth treaty, which, although nearly completed, remained a work in progress when he died. In the face of skepticism and outright opposition to the Maa-nulth Nations' agreement to a treaty with the governments of British Columbia and Canada, Evan's passion to see his First Nation participate in the umbrella treaty was staunch.

Shortly after the Yuułuʔiłʔatḥ First Nation approved entering into the Maa-nulth treaty, and just a few weeks before his death, Evan was invited to speak at a community gathering of the Tsawwassen First Nation on British Columbia's Lower Mainland.[14] (Tsawwassen community members were considering the implications of entering into their own treaty, and were anxious to hear from someone whose First Nation had already approved an agreement.) The young man—tanned, with neatly cut hair and an open-necked business shirt—stood and spoke passionately and with complete candour. It was almost as if he knew it was his last chance to speak to his beliefs and truths.

This is what he had to say:

> I'm fairly new to the formal treaty process, to tell the truth. I've just been elected as a band councillor, following in the footsteps of my brother Tyson.
>
> If I go back about twelve years ago, I guess you would say at that time I was anti-treaty. But what changed how I see the way a treaty affects our people was something an elder said to me.
>
> I was maybe twenty or twenty-one at the time. I wasn't one of those young guys who wore camouflage jumpsuits and long braids, you know. I looked a lot like I look now. But I was at a community meeting and I spoke hard and loud against what I

14 See "Standing on Our Own Two Feet," page 104.

thought was treaty, what I believed in then were our Aboriginal rights. I said to them, "What you are getting in this treaty is not enough for me." One of the councillors replied to me, "Well, what is enough?" I replied, "I think I'm worth a million bucks."

I was serious too. I wasn't thinking about what our people had lost in the past, I was only thinking about what I wanted to gain for myself. I wasn't thinking about our land and what we can't do with our own land, or what we can do with treaty. I never thought about what we don't have. I didn't realize I was sitting in a building that wasn't owned by our First Nation—it was owned by the Department of Indian Affairs [DIA]. Nothing was ours, unless we were to go through the treaty process.

What changed me was an elder who was there. She sat down and she looked at me and she said, "You know what? It's about more than money. It's about how we lived before, how we governed ourselves, our traditions. We all had roles in our community and we still do. I have one of those roles now. I hate calling myself a politician, but I am. We're not the same as 130 years ago, but we still have those roles to play." This elder pointed that out to me, and she showed me that this is what our treaty is all about.

I know everyone has a different perspective about what treaty is all about. Mine is: it's all about freedom. Freedom to do what you want, with your lands, freedom either to be a bum or to prosper.

I was a bum for ten years. I'll tell you the truth: I surfed and did nothing. I wanted the government to look after me. I wanted the government to pay me off, to give me a million bucks and then go away, and that's what I thought treaty was back then. Now I've woken up. Now it's about my tyee, *my chief, and my beliefs. I have three boys that I sit here for. If you look ahead twenty-five years after treaty, by the time they have children, those kids will be okay. But if we go the DIA route, nothing will change.*

The way I see it, we're held down by the Indian Act. *That line*

Evan Touchie's vision for the future was one of prosperity, well-being and independence for the next generation, including his beloved sons. *Courtesy Melody Charlie*

that is the reserve boundary—and I hate the word "reserve"— I'm First Nation, this is a First Nations community. "Reserve" is not our word—it's a DIA word.

I'm really outspoken when it comes to treaty. I tell our people, my DIA number is 668001R43501. What other place or community do you know where you have a number? Jails, institutions, residential schools—these are the only places you see where people have numbers. That's no different than a status card. I'd rather be free than have a number. If I could have an ID card that said, "This is my First Nation, this is my name," that would mean more to me than getting status-card gas and smokes.

I'm not highly educated. I have Grade 12, that's it. My brother has a BA in business and my mom, Bernice, has a doctorate. My uncle is a lawyer. I don't have that technical knowledge. I can't explain the technicalities of the treaty like they can. But I go on the road and I talk about tradition, and what it feels like to think about freedom. I can explain freedom. Freedom to do what you want and not what the government wants. Both my parents are politicians. I was brought up on red tape. Right now getting permission to do anything on reserve is crazy.

You know, we shocked everyone when we told the government we were ready for a treaty. People think we aren't ready for a treaty, but we're getting educated and we know what to do. And when will we be ready? The land is disappearing around us. If we wait it will all be gone.

I have a young, really educated friend, he's anti-treaty. He reminds me of how I was at that age. He says we're not ready. But I say to him, "Who's going to get us a better treaty?" We had a great team of people working for our treaty.

We couldn't be more ready than we are. We had to take this step. We had to shrug off the naysayers and take the risk. We are ready, and I'd rather be free.

Evan Touchie will always be missed by Melody; his mother, Bernice; his family; his friends; and the many other people who admired and loved him, both within the Yuułuʔiłʔatḥ First Nation and further afield.

Thoughts from Bonnie Leonard

b. 1966

Tk'emlúps First Nation

Tribal Director, Shuswap Nation Tribal Council

(interviewed in 2004)

If there's one thing that I believe more strongly than anything else, it's the children who are going to lead Aboriginal communities into a better future.

I hope to see the day when all First Nations in Canada have taken back the care and well-being of their children and families from government, and are revitalizing the old traditional lessons, practices and stories. I'm a firm believer in education and practices consistent with the teachings of the Elders.

The most important thing is to get children young—really young, between two and five years of age—and teach them responsibility right from the start. My kids, they don't get anything unless they work for it. That's important to me. All children should learn that, no matter who they are.

The kids are everyone's future. If we want them to grow up strong, we all have to bring them up right.

Photo courtesy Bonnie Leonard

14: Only One Lifetime

Things have come a long way since my father's day. We've gone from him being utterly marginalized to someone like me being able to run for the highest political office in the land if I want to. But there's still so much more work to do to make things really change for the better. There's only so much that can be done in one lifetime, but that's what I want to spend mine doing.

Troy Sebastian, b. 1976
Ktunaxa Nation, East Kootenays
Former political candidate and treaty negotiator
Political commentator
Law student
Good son

Troy Sebastian's favourite coffee hangout in the provincial capital, where he is a law student at the University of Victoria, is Discovery Coffee on the Fernwood/Oak Bay border. He prefers it to any of the campus options. Besides, Troy says, "I like the vinyl." He means the music, not the decor: Troy, an amateur musician in what little spare time he can find, is a drummer from way back.

The café is busy, and he waves to several acquaintances as they come in the door. At one point he leaps up to invite a couple at another table to Thanksgiving dinner the following weekend.

Troy Sebastian
Courtesy BC NDP

Apologizing for the interruption, he explains: "All those big holiday dinners, they're important to me. I love them. They're always a lot of fun." After glancing at his watch—his mother is visiting from the Okanagan, and he wants to make sure he gets home in time to make her breakfast when she wakes up—he returns to the topic at hand, his love of politics. "Politics," he says with deep reverence, "is in my heart and soul."

Indeed, Troy Sebastian is a political creature from head to toe. As a young man undertaking his undergraduate degree at Camosun College in Victoria—in political studies, naturally—he flung himself into student affairs with gusto. In 2001, at the tender age of twenty-four, he ran unsuccessfully for the provincial legislature under the banner of the BC New Democratic Party. Undaunted, he repeated the attempt in 2009. Although he lost again he was undismayed, seeing both campaigns as valuable learning experiences for a future career in politics.

He's had a stint as president of the St. Mary's Indian Band Education Council on his home reserve near Cranbrook in the East Kootenays, and spent five years on the board of governors of the College of the Rockies—sitting as chair in the final year. Moving back to Victoria in 2011 to study law didn't slow Troy down. He remains vice-president of the Native Courtworker and Counselling Association of British Columbia, on whose board of directors he has been an active member for several years. He has also been sharing his often-controversial opinions on *Public Eye*, a weekly political panel hosted by CFAX, a local Victoria radio station.

This political bent of his goes back as far as he can remember. His parents, Patricia and Mark Sebastian, introduced him to their world of social activism and politics when he was a wide-eyed five-year-old. The new federal Constitution was about to be implemented, and night after night around the dinner table they discussed its implications and the recognition and affirmation of the long-standing rights of the Aboriginal peoples of Canada, after so many years of denial. The little boy could barely understand the conversation but instinctively knew that what they were saying was vitally important. As an adult, its significance is firmly entrenched in his psyche.

It is a legacy for which he is immensely grateful to his parents, along with every other aspect of his socially active upbringing. Throughout his childhood Troy also accompanied his mother, a Scots Canadian hailing from Cape Breton, on numerous political engagements supporting various causes. Many of them were related to women's rights and well-being.

"My mom was very engaged in the women's rights movement. Not that long ago I saw a photograph of me when I was a little kid, holding a placard up at some gathering with 'Women's Equality' pasted all over it," he says. "I looked at her and asked her, 'So where do you think I get this from, eh?' She laughed," he recalls fondly.

What he learned from his mother about the importance of advocating for women is another valuable gift. "Women are the foundation of our well-being," he says simply. "If women are respected and treated well, children prosper. Yet thousands upon thousands of women in British Columbia live in poverty. Aboriginal women in particular are among the most marginalized people in the country. It's not surprising that there are more Aboriginal children in state care now than there were during the residential-school era. That's simply and utterly wrong," he says adamantly, "and that has got to change."

The opportunity to effect social transformation through political involvement, even though his views on how to do that have evolved over the last couple of years, is something he embraces with gratitude and wonderment at how much has changed for First Nations people in even one generation. He is lucky, he says: his Ktunaxa father, Mark, never imagined doing what his son has undertaken. "My father died in 1984, and never got the chance to witness my campaigns," says Troy, the loss of his father still weighing heavily on his shoulders. "There's been so much change in the last few decades, it's astounding," he continues. "I don't know if he could have imagined that one day I would actually stand for election to the provincial government."

Troy is devoted to his mother, Patricia, who has been a loving and significant influence in his life. *Courtesy Troy Sebastian*

When the Canadian Constitution was finally enacted in 1982, Mark Sebastian was already fifty-eight years old. He had served as an elected politician for several years on the St. Mary's Indian Band Council. But as a status Indian under the *Indian Act,* he had only been allowed to vote in British Columbia's provincial elections for the first time in 1949, at the age of twenty-five: the first time since European colonization that any status Indian in British Columbia had participated in the province's democratic process.

The provincial government's decision to allow the Aboriginal franchise at last may have been stimulated in part by guilt. Despite the fact that Canada did not recognize them as citizens, thousands of First Nations men and women had signed up to participate in Canada's armed forces to defend the country during the Second

World War. But if shame was the reason for the change, Canada apparently did not share any such sense of remorse, at least immediately. Mark Sebastian would be thirty-six before he would finally be allowed to vote in a federal election in Canada, in 1960. "I sometimes wonder," Troy muses, "what he would have thought about my running for the provincial legislature."

At the time Troy ran for office, it was in large part because of the reality that First Nations communities continue to face severe challenges. Decisions that affect First Nations people were—and still are—being made by government every day. But while there are strong First Nations political and advocacy organizations that tackle the government head-on about those decisions, Troy realized that not one single elected First Nations individual within the government was involved in making those decisions in the first place.

While he at first considered running for his band council like his father before him, Troy eventually rejected the idea. "I thought that these were basic challenges that everyone in the province should be addressing," he says. "That meant bringing them to people's attention in a much bigger forum. Good decisions about First Nations' rights and real reconciliation would also benefit everyone in BC, not just Aboriginal people. Those are the reasons I thought I wanted to be in the provincial government, rather than just a local politician."

Troy's reasons were also personal. "I had three brothers who have all passed away," he says in a matter-of-fact tone that belies the shocking revelation. "My father lost three sons. I can't even begin to imagine that misery." One brother, John, was killed by a drunk driver. The youngest of the three, J.R., succumbed to drug addiction when Troy was nineteen. Kenny simply disappeared. All of his brothers, considerably older than him—they were already young adults by the time he was born—lived lives of societal marginalization and despair.

"My life could have been like that too," he reflects. "I keep going back to that place where my brother J.R. died on the Downtown

Eastside in Vancouver—twenty-eight years later it's no better, and in fact I think it's become worse. We have to confront this!" he exclaims passionately. "My brother's story compels me to do something. I don't want to get to the end of my life and think that I didn't do enough to change this situation."

It was when Troy enrolled at Camosun College that the political light bulb really went on for the first time. "I had moved to Victoria in 1996 and initially had to be on welfare because I had nothing and couldn't get a job. I eventually found a midnight shift doing hotel laundry. It was anything but a good way to be living. That's when I figured out I needed to go back to school," he says.

He quickly became active in student politics, eventually chairing the University of Victoria Students' Society and taking on the job of national Aboriginal representative on the Canadian Students' Federation. Troy also made friends who would remain influential in his choice of career, including future BC New Democrat Party MLA Rob Fleming, then a fellow student. "My first campaign poster was made on Rob's computer," he recalls fondly. "I learned so much from him. He was an amazing inspiration to me." Former BC NDP leader Carole James was another strong role model, and remains a friend he admires and respects greatly.

After completing his BA in history and political science at UVic in 2005, Troy returned to St. Mary's to work for the Ktunaxa Nation as a treaty negotiator. After the 2009 provincial election, he fully intended to run again in 2013, hoping the third time would prove lucky. But in 2010 everything changed. A short news release announced his decision: the disillusioned aspiring politician was resigning from the BC NDP.

While it was difficult to part political ways with old friends, leaving the party itself was easy, Troy says. After fourteen years of active involvement, he had become increasingly aware that nothing was changing to improve the lives of indigenous people in British Columbia—and that the provincial NDP itself was part of the problem. "The indifference and privilege that the party demonstrates toward indigenous peoples is shameful," he wrote in his letter of resignation. "The party is bereft of understanding of the issue and complacent toward any notion of change."

Troy had hoped to achieve some positive steps toward social justice for all British Columbians as part of a provincial NDP government, but not at the cost of ignoring the pressing plight of First Nations people. With no evidence that the party was willing to step up to the plate on indigenous issues, he felt increasingly compromised. Finally he reached the limit of his tolerance, writing: "I can no longer subsume my indigenousness in order to be a member of this party." He never received a response.

Two years later, his thinking has evolved even further. He now characterizes the whole system, not just one party or the other, as a vehicle for fundamentally flawed colonial politics. "When I ran for office, I wanted to see what difference a First Nations MLA could make. The jury's still out on that, of course, but I suspect not much." Troy points to what he calls the "failed experiment" of federal Health Minister Leona Aglukkaq, the first Inuk to become a member of the federal cabinet and the subject of widespread criticism for toeing the Conservative Party line rather than standing with her people against detrimental government policy. "It's just not a good system for indigenous people," he says. "Heck, it's not good for most Canadians. This system doesn't work for *any* of us. Why would it be any better for First Nations?"

While you can take the boy out of politics, you can't take the politics out of the boy. "I still consume it constantly," he admits. "I can't help myself!" The only difference is that now he gets to critique it from the outside—and he's not afraid to say what he thinks in the bluntest of terms. "Some people think I'm unnecessarily antagonistic," he says. "But I just see it as speaking the truth. That can be pretty intense sometimes." The topic of reconciliation between First Nations and non-indigenous people is a good example: "Canada's history with First Nations is a national embarrassment," Troy says unequivocally. "Some people don't like to hear that, but things need to change, and platitudes won't help."

Troy agrees wholeheartedly that the gulf between indigenous

and non-indigenous Canadians needs to be closed. But, he says frankly, he has yet to see any meaningful gesture on the part of non-indigenous Canadians to do that. In the meantime First Nations are getting tired of reconciliation being effectively a one-way street in which they are expected to give up their rights and receive little in return. "That's not reconciliation."

He believes change has to come at a fundamental level, requiring a cultural and philosophical shift and an honesty that are both currently missing in action. "The problems of indigenous peoples are well known now," Troy says. "We know that if they get solved things will be better for everyone. But where's the hue and cry from the Canadian public about solving our problems? I don't hear it yet."

Troy thinks several things need to happen for that to change: "First and foremost, there needs to be a complete re-examination at a foundational level of the whole basis of the relationship between the state and indigenous peoples in Canada, because that's the basis for the position we find ourselves in today."

The colonizers of Canada, he continues, created a founding narrative that still promotes the concept that they arrived in an "unsettled land," empty of any civilized peoples. "They defined civilization by technological knowledge or business acumen rather than by the traditional wisdom with which First Nations have governed themselves since time immemorial—certainly since before the Magna Carta, the founding document of Western governance. Instead they characterized the First Nations societies they encountered as savage and uncivilized. They said we weren't even people."

That, says Troy, is the fundamental basis on which the state constructed and manifested its relationship with First Nations, and from which Canadian settlers and their descendants have taken their cue ever since. "So that's the legacy we live with today. That is still the reality of indigenous people in Canada. We still have governments denying we're people in court, and trying to prevent us from governing ourselves and employing our own cultural traditions and wisdom for healthy societies. We still have businesses reaping vast profits from the resources in our territories with no recognition that we have been the stewards of those resources for thousands of years before settlers arrived. It's a fundamentally flawed relationship that has to be taken apart and reconstructed from the beginning, and everyone," he says adamantly, "has to buy into that for it to work. We need people to accept what happened, learn about the consequences and accept the differences. That's what reconciliation means."

Another vital step is to overcome stereotypes, and what he describes as systemic racism that slots First Nations people into predetermined roles and outcomes. That takes more than simply putting an end to the labelling of Indians as lazy, or shiftless, or drunks, although that's a basic step to take too. Telling an Aboriginal person to get over a past of injustice, racism, active discrimination and outright abuse is also immensely hurtful. What, he would like to know, is he supposed to be getting over, exactly?

A sense of humour helps. "Fundamentally, I'm proud of my heritage and it helps to tell people about it," he explains. "I like to say to them, 'It's true that part of my background comes from a community that likes to eat strange foods, has a history of living off the land, going into combat with war paint on their faces and fighting the English. But you know," he concludes with a straight face, "the Scottish have their good points too.'"

The treaty process, he says more sombrely, has done little to help improve life for First Nations in British Columbia. "I was thrilled when the modern-day process was announced back in 1991. It was great. True reconciliation between First Nations and the rest of British Columbia was finally on the way, and it would be achieved by the time I finished high school!" Troy was enthusiastic enough about the potential of the process for reconciliation that even when it became clear that treaty-making was going to take quite a bit longer than that, he joined his First Nations' treaty negotiation team as the director of the lands and resources portfolio.

Now he says, "I think the process has completely failed.

Government has no real interest in settling with us. Canada and British Columbia have not been negotiating in good faith for years. That's not likely to change. They want what they call economic certainty and the extinguishment or limitation of our rights. I'm in favour of getting away from the Department of Indian Affairs, but that's not the answer. We have to be able to exercise our rights, not let go of them in exchange for a few dollars that amount to a fraction of the value of what has been taken from us." The worst thing about it, he reflects, is the loss of hope and opportunity. "It could have made such a difference."

On other fronts, things have generally changed for the better for First Nations people of his generation. Canadian case law has made it clear to governments in the past thirty years that they can no longer simply ride roughshod over Aboriginal rights, whether or not treaties are in place. Governments have also become increasingly open to economic development partnerships and management-sharing protocols over Crown lands. The Columbia River Treaty between Canada and the United States, governing the use of water in the river as it flows through the heart of Ktunaxa traditional territory and across the border, is due for renegotiation during this decade. That offers his people potential for a beneficial compensation agreement with governments to accommodate their rights and interests in the river.

His long-term goal after he graduates is to head back home to work for the Ktunaxa people to keep making progress on matters such as these. "We're a minority, and we can't compel change, at least not using the methods we've been trying to use. But we can tell the government to stop telling us who and what we are and what we can do. We can govern ourselves now, without approval from the state, and that's what we should be doing."

Ktunaxa people, like other First Nations, have to work in their own language traditions to be culturally strong and independent of colonial systems that create regimes like the *Indian Act* and promulgate welfare dependence. "It's what we have to do if we want to be healthy and whole like we were before colonization. We need to have what other Canadians take for granted, and we have to do it for ourselves."

One of the many things Ktunaxa have been doing is fighting to preserve Qat'muk, a sacred grizzly bear spirit area, from potential development as a ski resort. In 2011, the Ktunaxa delivered what is known as the Qat'muk Declaration to provincial leaders on the steps of the Legislature. The declaration outlines the cultural significance of Qat'muk, and principles for its use and protection. Delivering it to the government was a watershed moment for Troy.

"We took the Ktunaxa flag with us," he says. "I remember the pride and the joy I felt standing there, and the realization that I was doing what I'm meant to do. I fought so hard to be an MLA, and there I was standing in the Legislature but holding the Ktunaxa

Troy signing the "Keep Jumbo Wild" banner at the Farnham Creek road blockade during the summer of 2008, protesting proposed resort development in an area sacred to the Ktunaxa. *Courtesy Troy Sebastian*

flag and representing the Ktunaxa people instead. It was an amazing feeling. It was so much more meaningful to me."

It would be a great day, acknowledges Troy, if it became unremarkable to see a First Nations MLA elected and governments making decisions in a socially responsible way that respect indigenous peoples. He doesn't know if he'll be around to see that happen. "Things have come a long way since my father's day," he concedes. "We've gone from him being utterly marginalized to someone like me being able to run for the highest political office in the land if I want to. But there's still so much more work to do to make things really change for the better."

He drains his coffee, and picks up his bicycle helmet. Time to go; his mom needs her breakfast. "I'm up for that work, though," he says as he turns to leave. "There's only so much that can be done in one lifetime, but that's what I want to spend mine doing."

15: Weathering All Storms

Yes, life has highs and lows. But sometimes the most valuable teachings come from the lows. You just have to hang on, hunker down and ride out the storm. No matter how tumultuous it may be, the storm inevitably passes and the sun comes out again, and you will be left stronger and wiser for that storm you just weathered.

Anne Tenning, b. 1975
Stz'uminus (Chemainus) First Nation, Ladysmith/Penticton
District principal, Aboriginal Education, Okanagan/Skaha
School District
BA (English, biology) and B.Ed. (secondary education)
MA, environmental and First Nations education (2010)
Daughter of a residential-school survivor
Writer, runner and Tragically Hip fan

Aspiring writer Anne Tenning is sitting across from me at the dining-room table of author Richard Wagamese, in his home near Kamloops, British Columbia. Anne and I are both unconsciously frowning, frantically typing on our laptop computers. While we write, Richard, who is seated between us at the table, is calmly reviewing a draft of *Indian Horse*, his latest novel.

It is June 2011, and day three of an intense five-day creative writing retreat with Richard, who is sharing his wisdom and experience about channelling creative energy into stories. Right now, Anne and I are releasing our creative energy through a free-form writing exercise. It is one of many we have already undertaken over the past seventy-two hours: we are both exhausted and

Anne Tenning, right, with her mother, Elizabeth Tenning.
Laura Leyshon photo

Anne at a writing workshop at the Kamloops home of celebrated author Richard Wagamese. The work required intense concentration and effort—but was also inspiring, and fun. *Katherine Palmer Gordon photo*

exhilarated at the same time, drained by the intense effort but bursting with inspiration as Richard unrelentingly lobs idea after idea at us to work on.

Despite the fact that we are both non-fiction writers, the writing exercises have resulted in unexpected bursts of fantasy and playfulness on our part. Perhaps that's because we are so tired. When Anne reads out what she has written—a dark tale involving a frog, a pond, a moonlit night and a hapless camper named Roger who meets a sticky end—we start laughing at her quirky prose and can't stop. When Richard's wife, Debra Powell, pokes her head around the corner to ask what on earth is going on, Anne blurts out: "Roger died!" We all roar again, lost in a moment of uninhibited, helpless, hilarious companionship of the kind we all too rarely enjoy in our adult lives.

All I knew about Anne when we met for the first time at the beginning of the retreat was that she was from the Stz'uminus First Nation on southern Vancouver Island, and that she was a teacher

(English and First Nations Studies) at Victoria High School. A quick internet search had revealed that in 2008 she won a prestigious Governor General's Award for Excellence in Teaching Canadian History. My companion and roommate for the duration of the retreat was clearly a smart cookie. I was initially wary about sharing a room for five days with a complete stranger, but Anne's down-to-earth nature and well-honed sense of humour endeared her to me immediately.

She told me she wanted to be a writer, but didn't say what she wanted to write about. The exercises we'd done didn't reveal anything in that respect, except that Anne clearly had an idiosyncratic imagination and an easy way with words. It wasn't until the last evening of the retreat that Richard, Debra and I all discovered just how inspired a writer Anne really is—and how important what she has to say is to every Canadian.

That evening, Richard invited us to read a completed story that we had been working on over the course of the past two days. Anne read an essay she had called "Weathering Storms." The three of us became utterly still as she started describing the experience of accompanying her mother to a federal government compensation hearing, held to look into the abuse her mother, Elizabeth, had experienced as a child in a church-run residential school on Kuper Island, near Chemainus on Vancouver Island.

The previous year the government had paid her mother, like other survivors, a small sum in notional compensation. To qualify for it, Elizabeth first had to prove she had attended the school. That wasn't easy, because the First Nation had since torn down the school, flinging some of its bricks into the sea in a symbolic attempt to erase the past. Elizabeth received the money in the end, but at the cost of reviving all the painful memories of being in the school—memories that she had previously managed to suppress for most of her adult life.

"My mother now had the residential school on her mind every time she went to the bank," Anne read out slowly, perched on a stool at the front of the room. She stopped to clear her throat from time to time as she described her mother's suffering. "She always now needed something to keep her busy and distracted from her thoughts. She couldn't sleep at night. She would be hit with waves of tears out of nowhere."

Residential-school survivors could choose to simply accept the small lump-sum payment and end the whole process there, or go further in the compensation process and tell their stories in detail at a full assessment inquiry, similar to a court hearing. For Anne's mother, tormented by her memories, it was impossible to say that it was over. She decided she should take that next step. "Nothing could have prepared me for that experience," recalled Anne.

Elizabeth's hearing was held in late 2008. November of that year was a see-saw experience for Anne: "One day, I was in Ottawa receiving my Governor General's award, feeling honoured and celebrated. Forty-eight hours later, I was at a hotel in Duncan, attending my mother's hearing." Anne was allowed only to listen, not to speak. What she heard was nothing short of horrifying.

"I knew virtually nothing about my mother's experience until then," Anne read. "For six long hours, I sat beside her as they questioned her: *tell us the ways and extent to which you were violated in residential school and the impact this has had on your life. You have to tell us everything. Don't leave a single detail out. Oh, and we will question you again and insinuate that what you are telling us is not real or true. We will make sure to resurface old demons that you haven't thought about for years. Oh yes, those scars will bleed once more.*

"My mother recounted all the abuses she suffered at the hands of school employees," Anne read quietly. "I listened silently, resisting the urge to scream, to cry, to vomit. The whole time, I wished I could hold my mother and somehow protect her from her own memories. My mother is a master at weathering the worst of storms in her life, as am I, but this day brought a storm like no other. Would she be able to hang on through the storm, in her little dinghy in the wild, open ocean? Would I? The waters were the roughest I'd felt in years, but I knew I could do it. I was terrified,

In 2008, Anne won a prestigious Governor General's Award for Excellence in Teaching Canadian History. Michaëlle Jean, then Governor General, presided over the ceremony. *Courtesy Anne Tenning*

but I knew my mother was strong and had survived moments that would have broken the hardiest of souls. As we each pushed off into the violence of the storm I held her hand, wept often, and at the end of the hearing felt so much admiration, love and respect for my mother. She stood up and thanked everyone, even the lawyers. Out of nowhere, she said she was proud of me. I understood who she is more completely than ever."

Her mother's heartbreaking story is one Anne continues to hold in her own heart and mind in her daily role as an educator, whether as a teacher of First Nations studies sharing lessons from colonial history with her students, or in her current role as district principal of Aboriginal Education in BC School District 67, based in Penticton. She believes it is vital for Canadians to know and understand the story of Canada's residential schools, and their impact on society. "For the First Nations of Canada, the term *residential school* is synonymous with a systemic attempt to eradicate Aboriginal culture and identity. Knowing that is pivotal to comprehending the issues facing Aboriginal people today. Children were not only treated with neglect, abuse and disrespect, the quality of education was minimal. Worst of all, children were essentially robbed of their childhoods and denied the basic rights of a child: to be loved, protected and cared for by their families."

The next generation also suffered at the hands of fathers and mothers who, deprived of a family upbringing, had never learned how to be parents. At times Anne juggled school and exams with 911 ambulance calls for her mother, who suffered from periodic bouts of depression. But she loved school, and managed to do well. After receiving her teaching degree from the University of British Columbia in 2000, Anne taught briefly in North Vancouver and at Stu"ate Lelum Secondary School in Ladysmith before moving to Victoria. Five years later she began her master's degree in environmental and First Nations education at the University of Victoria, and her passion for teaching First Nations culture and history was ignited.

An immensely popular teacher at Victoria High, Anne would introduce her students to the writing of acclaimed First Nations writers like Richard Wagamese, and expose to them traditional methods of learning through talking circles—even when the only option to create a talking circle around a "fire" in her classroom was to use a plastic replica of an outdoor fireplace bought from Walmart. "I'm not sure I was really allowed to light the candles in the classroom, but the students loved it!" Anne chuckles.

It was with strong dismay therefore that they learned that one of their favourite teachers was moving to Penticton in January 2012, to take on a new job in the Okanagan/Skaha School District. It was an offer she hadn't been able to turn down. "It was very much the right time for me," she says. "I felt like it was a good point in my life to make a move. I'd finished my master's degree, and I had been keeping an eye out for a position in the Okanagan in particular. My twin sister, Kathy, lives in Vernon, and I was travelling a lot to see her. It was getting harder and harder not to be around as my nephew Bryce, who is now eighteen, and my niece Leandra, who is fourteen, were growing up."

A posting for a counsellor had come up, but she had felt it wasn't the right fit for her. The school district was so taken with her résumé, however, that they created a new position, district vice-principal, that was tailor-made for Anne's unique skills and experience. She accepted on the spot. "As district vice-principal, I oversaw fourteen staff in the Aboriginal Education program. That program offers support to Aboriginal students and cultural enrichment as part of the curricula. I was also the key liaison person between the school district and our partner agencies, like the Penticton Indian Band, the Métis Association, the Friendship Centres and other community agencies like the En'owkin Centre. I coordinated meetings and projects with our partners. It was a really big role, and it was exactly what I wanted to be doing."

All the same, it was a role she took on with both trepidation and excitement. It meant moving away from classroom teaching and the students she loved, as well as from Victoria and all her friends and family, to Penticton—a town she had visited only a couple of times before and where she knew absolutely nobody. "It was January, and so cold and dry, nothing like the coast. I felt like I had been parachuted onto another planet!"

She didn't allow herself any time to mope. Her adored but demanding cat, Bandit, was there to keep her company and distract her. "It was also so great being nearer to my sister and her kids. I made sure I kept myself busy when I wasn't working too. I spent a lot more time writing. I learned how to make earrings, and I finally finished a monumental scrapbook I had started from a trip to Germany I had taken in the summer of 2010."

Anne has had a German pen-pal, Daniela, since she was twelve years old. "I had a wonderful teacher called Mrs. Clark, who taught the Aboriginal Resource Room at George Jay Elementary in Victoria. Mrs. Clark was like a second mother to me. She asked me and my sister if we would like to write to her nieces in Germany,

Anne has been pen-pals with her German friend Daniela for more than twenty-five years. *Courtesy Anne Tenning*

who were about the same age as us. It's just as well that Dani and I paired up, because my sister and Dani's sister only ever wrote to each other once—they weren't that interested in writing. But Dani and I have been writing to each other ever since, telling each other about our lives, how things were going, what was happening with us. We've done it for more than twenty-five years now."

Her 2010 visit to Germany was the first time that Anne and Daniela met in person. "I was very nervous about how it would go. But we'd grown up together, through our letters. We really knew each other. From the minute we met we were long-lost sisters who had found each other—it was very natural. There was no awkwardness at all." Anne's scrapbook records a joyful and emotional three weeks with her friend. "One of the most memorable moments was when Daniela brought out a box containing every letter and card I had ever written to her," Anne recalls. "It was overwhelming! There was this whole record of my life over the last twenty-five years—what I was thinking when I was thirteen, seventeen, twenty-five—it was all there."

Anne was thrilled by the love and thoughtfulness that the gesture represented, but couldn't bring herself to read the letters at that stage. "I will sit down one day and read them all. I have hers, too, for her to read eventually. We will have to do something with them together, I think. There's so much there." In 2011 Daniela came to visit Anne in Canada, bringing her husband, Oliver, with her; 2013 was Anne's turn for a return trip to Germany, this time to see Daniela and Oliver's baby son. There is a bond of friendship between the two women that promises to bring a lifetime of journeys between their two countries.

In April 2012, Anne decided she wanted to get into shape and improve her health. "I was motivated to get started by a keynote speech that I was going to be giving at the Victoria High School graduation ceremony in June 2012, in front of an audience of a thousand people at the University of Victoria auditorium. It was the same stage that I walked across during my high school graduation ceremony in June 1993, and again in June 2010 during my master's convocation. I had graduated from Victoria High School nineteen years earlier, and I was going to be speaking in front of my former colleagues and students with whom I had worked while I was a teacher at Vic High. I wanted to present to them the best version of myself, which meant I needed to change my lifestyle and get healthier. I had ten weeks to do it, and it worked!"

Anne dug out what she describes as her "sadly neglected" gym clothes and shoes and started running three times a week. Penticton's spring felt as warm as a Victoria summer, and watching other runners jogging along the shore of nearby Okanagan Lake had enticed her out of doors to try it for herself. "It was hard work but I loved it! I lost twenty pounds and felt completely different, not just physically but in myself as a person. I have far more energy, I suffer less from stress and I feel very positive." Even the Okanagan winter could not deter her. In January 2013 she signed up for a two-month running clinic with the goal of undertaking the annual Vancouver Sun Run. "It was awesome! My running skills really improved. The bonus was I met people with a lot in common—they had moved to Penticton from somewhere else, they had maybe had a hard time building a social network, and they were into long-distance running."

Anne also gets social time at the monthly "soirees" that Richard Wagamese and Debra Powell host at their home, a couple of hours' drive from Penticton. Guests are invited to offer a reading, some musical entertainment, or anything arts-related that they wish to perform. Anne goes as often as she can, using the opportunity to read out her latest writing efforts to an appreciative audience. Roger's story has evolved and grown, finally coming to an end in early 2013—with great reluctance on Anne's part to let go of the characters she had created and come to love.

"I felt like a geek getting all teary at the soiree when I read the ending of the final instalment! What am I going to do without Roger, Michelle, Matthias and Scott?" she wonders. She's left open the possibility of a sequel, nonetheless. The story currently ends this way: "Somewhere a frog sits perched on a log in the darkness of the night, observing every little movement in and around the pond with his ever-watchful eyes, and he wonders to himself…" Watch this space.

Anne's work as an educator remains her passion. In May 2013 she was promoted to the position of district principal of Aboriginal Education in the Okanagan/Skaha School District. She stays in touch with many of her former students from Victoria, and has made sure she still gets in some classroom time, even in her new job. "I still love interacting with students, so once a week I co-facilitate an after-school tutorial for elementary students, and I also guest-teach when I can, especially to keep educating the students about the residential-school story."

Anne with her beloved twin sister, Kathy, at Anne's graduation. *Aaron Parker photo*

It's a story that Anne feels a duty to keep telling for the sake of all the survivors, but especially her mother, whose trials were not over after the initial six-hour hearing. If she wanted to continue in the compensation process to its conclusion, she would have to tell her story again at yet more sessions. But by that stage Elizabeth was determined to see it through to the end.

"My mom said to all of us, 'You're damn right I'm taking the next step! I've come this far, haven't I?'" Anne wrote. "Then she smiled, and I knew she would be OK. That's my mom. She's four foot eleven, but she has a giant's share of strength. She taught me to weather storms that no one else can see.

"I am so grateful she asked me to be there that day. That day changed my life. It changed my understanding of my mother. For the first time, all the pieces came flying together. It changed my understanding of my sisters, of myself. Yes, life has highs and lows. But sometimes the most valuable teachings come from the lows. You just have to hang on, hunker down and ride out the storm. No matter how tumultuous it may be, the storm inevitably passes and the sun comes out again, and you will be left stronger and wiser for that storm you just weathered."

Thoughts from Adam Olsen

b. 1976

Tsartlip First Nation

Politician (Central Saanich councillor from 2008 to 2013; Green Party candidate for Saanich North and the Islands in 2013 provincial election)

(interviewed in 2007)

Courtesy Adam Olsen

I grew up with an identity crisis. I'm half-First Nations, half-white. As a kid, to each side I was the other. I always had one leg either side of this invisible line that society had drawn for me.

Now, as an adult, I see that as empowering instead. It gives me the opportunity to play a very important role, because I'm comfortable in both worlds, working in my community and outside it. I can be a catalyst for the two sides to learn to live together. Really, they don't have any choice—neither side can deny the other side of me. I exist. I've learned to say comfortably this is where I belong.

16: Working Really Hard Just to Get to a Normal Place

Sometimes I look at the young actors, and they all want to be big stars. I always want to tell them: "Well, if you work really hard, you will get to be a professional actor. Once in a while, you might win the lottery and get big accolades for something you've done. But most of the time, you should just count on having to work really hard—not being a star—and most of the time, you can count on just being in a normal place."

Evan Tlesla Adams, b. 1966

Sliammon First Nation, Powell River/Vancouver

Actor and playwright

Doctor of medicine, University of Calgary, 2002

Master's in public health, Johns Hopkins Bloomberg School of Public Health

Deputy provincial health officer for British Columbia, Aboriginal Health

Very hard worker

If you just took his life at face value, it would be easy to think that Evan Adams is simply one heck of a lucky guy.

He holds one of the province's most senior medical jobs in his dream field of Aboriginal health. He is internationally respected for his work related to indigenous public well-being. He has five growing sons (and a stepdaughter), a large and loving extended family, 4,624 Facebook friends at last count, and (although his Facebook page doesn't mention it) he is currently in a long-term relationship. He is also fit and healthy; thanks to a lifelong love of running, staying in good shape comes naturally to this slim, slightly built man. If all that doesn't prove he drew a winning hand in the poker game of life, there is more: Evan is also a celebrated film and television star.

One day, when he was just eighteen years old and in the midst of his second year of undergraduate science studies at McGill University in Montreal, he decided to take a break and go out for a walk. Mid-stroll, he paused to look idly through the window of an acting agency. The owner came out and asked him if he was an actor. He wasn't, but for some inexplicable reason he said yes. The next day, he landed a lead role in a movie.

That chance encounter led to a professional acting career that has garnered him numerous international awards in both television and filmmaking circles, for roles such as Thomas Builds-the-Fire in the 1998 movie *Smoke Signals* and Seymour Polatkin in *The Business of Fancydancing*, released in 2002. He's appeared in many well-known Canadian TV series, including *The Beachcombers* and *Da Vinci's Inquest*. His stage roles have also been acclaimed, and have encompassed everything from Shakespeare to Tomson Highway's *Dry Lips Oughta Move to Kapuskasing*. His own plays have also met with critical success in Canada and abroad.

Yes, Evan is undoubtedly a lucky guy. He loves acting and appreciates the incredible experiences he has enjoyed in that profession. But luck is one thing; hard work is another. As the saying goes, the harder he's worked, the luckier Evan's got. His acting success is the reward for decades of study and commitment to his roles. In 2002,

Evan Adams
Courtesy Evan Adams

in between the almost constant film and television projects that he was actively involved in, Evan added a medical degree from the University of Calgary to his professional portfolio. He practised family medicine in Vancouver, served as director of the division of Aboriginal people's health at the University of British Columbia's Faculty of Medicine, and added a master's of public health (MPH) from Johns Hopkins University to his title. Oh yes, and he still acts and writes.

"I know I *am* privileged," Evan says thoughtfully. "I understand that. But I hope people realize that it was more than luck. Yes,

Evan attributes who he is today in large part to his upbringing by parents, Leslie and Mary Jane Adams. *Courtesy Grace Adams*

I feel immensely rich to have received the kind of upbringing I had, for one thing. My mother was very bright and well educated and made sure I also received the best education possible. She had me learning French from the age of four. When I decided to take biology and physics, she said, 'Of course you can do that,' even if none of the other kids were doing it." Evan also benefited greatly from his father's wisdom and experience: "He was the one who taught me how to work like a man. That was important to him. I understand that now when I see men who take on responsibility as opposed to those men who want to pretend they are still boys."

His father, Leslie, grew up in a traditional way, Evan says. "My dad's mother was only fourteen when she had him. She died of tuberculosis within weeks of giving birth, so his grandmother took him to raise him in the old ways. She taught him to hunt, to fish, and to survive in all weathers without anyone to help him." In turn, Leslie shared that traditional knowledge with Evan from his earliest childhood, taking him out on the land and teaching him the skills he believed his young son would one day need to provide for himself and his family. "He always told me the land and waters were our birthright."

But it was also a birthright that had to be earned; and his hands-on education was anything but easy. "My father insisted on rigorous discipline and a lot of hard work. He demanded that I be a good person. He said to me, 'You're a man, and you have to do these things. Who doesn't want to lie around all day? Who doesn't want to sleep in? We all want that, but you can't do it. You have to feed your family. There are old people who need you. There are young people who are growing up without someone to tell them what to do, and you have to help them.' He was very tough, but that's how he made me understand that I *had* to work hard at whatever I was doing, whether it was something I wanted to do, or that I simply should be doing because that was the right thing."

When he was fifteen years old, Leslie was captured by government authorities who took him away to residential school. There he met Evan's mother, Mary Jane, who had been in the school since the age of three. The two young people fell passionately in love, despite their very different upbringings. "She was very well educated and acculturated in the ways of the dominant culture, but she knew nothing about how to look after herself out on the land, in the old ways. Being in residential school had deprived her of that important knowledge. When they were married, she didn't even know how to boil a fish. She didn't know to cut out the gills— that's how little she knew," Evan says. His father was determined that Evan would never be disadvantaged in that way. "That's why, from the time I was very small, he took me out on the land to teach me the things he thought any person—not just an Aboriginal person, but anyone—should know about how to take care of themselves, and how to be strong of body and mind."

Leslie taught Evan many physical skills, but he also taught him the all-important lesson that, ultimately, disciplining his mind was what was most essential for strength, fitness and survival. "Running and cold-water bathing were two ways he taught me how to control my mind," recalls Evan. "Running was very good for developing willpower to overcome pain and exhaustion. Getting used to being in cold water was vital for diving and swimming for fish and other animals in all kinds of weather." For Evan's father, exercising self-control was simply part of growing up the Aboriginal way. "Our people always used to expect our children to be able to endure hardships like pain, hunger or loss without complaining. It was one of our virtues."

Colonization, Evan says sadly, has changed that. Enduring hardship to overcome adversity isn't as much a part of the mindset anymore for young people. Expectations have become high in twenty-first-century society that things should come easier. "Sometimes I look at the young actors, and they all want to be big stars. I always want to tell them: 'Well, if you work really hard, you will get to be a professional actor. Once in a while, you might win the lottery and get big accolades for something you've done. But most of the time, you should just count on having to work really hard—not being a star—and most of the time, you can count on just being in a normal place.' I don't know sometimes how to tell people to change their expectations. None of us gets out of this life without heartbreak, pain, or even occasional discomfort!" he exclaims. "These things are going to happen. But they *can* be overcome, with strength of mind and discipline—by learning to be resilient."

That's a lesson that Evan received at a young age, and in the hardest of possible ways. When he was nearly six years old, a tragic event occurred in his life, one that would be partly responsible for shaping his future path. "My sister was shot and killed in a hunting accident right in front of me, near our house. It was very horrific to witness." Even harder to witness was his parents' sorrow. "The experience of seeing my parents nearly die from grief was enormous. Everything else in my life was nothing by comparison." Evan barely remembers anything else from that time. "I do remember us struggling just to carry on living. I remember my mother's terrible sadness, and my father trying not to just withdraw into work but to stay present with us."

Time, of course, heals most wounds. "We did get better eventually. My parents made that happen as much as anything. They loved each other passionately all their lives," he explains. "They loved their children very much too. My father believed that if you love someone, you dedicate yourself completely to them. You don't abandon them or leave them behind, even when times are bad or you are feeling weak. So I could see, even as a child, even though they were at their weakest point, my parents were trying hard to get better, for their sake and for our sake. One day, we all realized we were recovering well at last. We made it past that terribly harsh time, and we survived."

The memory of that terrible day will never be erased, however. More than forty years later, despite having been so young at the time, Evan can still describe in graphic terms how terribly his sister died. The experience was one of his motivations for becoming a doctor. He had other reasons too: not only his grandmother but many other relatives had died of TB. He adds: "It was clear to me that we deserved better lives, and maybe with the skills of a doctor, I might be able to help."

At age fifteen, after spending a year at St. Michael's University School in Victoria, Evan won a scholarship to study at Lester B. Pearson College of the Pacific, an international school also located in Victoria. "There were students there from more than eighty countries. Many of them were from developing nations that were much poorer than Canada. They all felt this huge responsibility to get an education so that they could do something to help their people. All they wanted was to go back and help their fellow citizens have a better life. That's exactly how I felt too." Evan graduated from Pearson College two years later with a bilingual international baccalaureate, and headed off to McGill to start his biochemistry studies in 1984. But with his unexpected shift into an acting career, he left McGill again within a year and moved back to Vancouver to study drama.

It might have seemed a strange decision for someone who had decided he wanted to do something that would help his people have better lives. But for Evan, the move was entirely consistent with that goal. Acting, he says, is holy work to him. "For me, acting was never about being part of the whole Hollywood thing. I saw it as a different way to lift up my people—as an opportunity to portray real Aboriginal people leading real lives, not some strange fantasy image that the dominant culture has of Indians. Hollywood is all about selling impossible dreams. I wanted no part of that. Our people deserve to be portrayed truthfully, as the complex, sophisticated, modern-and-traditional people they are. That takes thoughtfulness and respect and real care."

Evan plunged into his new acting career with what had already become his trademark discipline. "In any of my roles, I always wanted to do my best for my people and to show how proud I am of them. I wanted to speak in the first person on their behalf and dispel myths and fantasies. To do that, I always had to make sure I worked as hard as possible to be true to the character I was playing, and be the best person for that job, not just play easy stereotypes or what other people thought the character should be."

In the role for which he is perhaps best known, *Smoke Signals'* Thomas Builds-the-Fire, Evan seized the opportunity to portray a young, modern Aboriginal man in a traditional way. "I didn't want to just surrender to the expectation that all young Indian men are too-cool-for-school and tough. So I decided to 'channel' the spirits of the most beautiful old Indian women I knew and share that traditional kind of character with people through Thomas. I wanted young people watching the film to see someone more like one of our ancestors—wise, very loving, dignified, funny and smart at the same time."

It worked: Evan's sweet, generous, hilariously geeky character

One of the better-known characters in Evan's acting portfolio is Thomas Builds-the-Fire (*Smoke Signals*). *Courtesy Evan Adams*

completely steals the show in the film. More importantly, as cultural myth-busting efforts go, Evan hit a home run with Thomas, a character who has endeared himself to both Aboriginal and non-Aboriginal audiences worldwide (the movie has screened in more than fifteen countries, including nations as diverse as Japan, Hungary and New Zealand, and has won countless awards).

As an actor, Evan says, the goal is to illuminate experiences. "Acting is meant not just to tell a story, but to share a story—to help the audience see the truth. It's not fakery. It's not about being pretty for the cameras, to be a star or to make lots of money. It's about bringing forward important ideas, and sharing experiences." That is immensely rewarding; it can also be immensely difficult. "I once played a gay man with HIV, for instance. When I was quite young, I played a boy who had been sexually abused. That's a terrible story, but by portraying that story faithfully and with real commitment, you can help others understand what that experience means, and empathize with it. I'm letting people know what being raped means without having to experience rape yourself. These Aboriginal lives and stories need to be put forward and shared," Evan repeats emphatically, "so that people will understand them better. There is still a huge need for that. There still aren't enough stories out there, onscreen or on the stage, telling the world about our lives."

After twelve years in the acting business, Evan's mind turned back to the medical career he had once contemplated. "I love acting, and I never want to have to give it up. It is just as important to me as being a doctor, in a different way. But when I turned twenty-nine, I started to feel I should be doing something more. I also realized that if I really did want to be a doctor, I would soon be too old to do the training required. It was now or never. So I decided to go back to school, finish my undergraduate work, and enrol in medical school. Everyone thought I was crazy."

Characteristically, diving into intensive medical studies didn't mean Evan slowed down on the acting front; he simply doubled his workload, flying off to film shoots and rehearsals in between exams. After receiving his medical degree in 2002, he returned to Vancouver once more to continue his family-medicine residency training. The transition was seamless. "There is a lot in common between acting and medicine for me. In both cases, it is all about really digging deep and asking the best of yourself and taking the best possible care. It makes a huge difference. If you don't truly believe that you can play this character, or help that person get better, then you won't."

Once again—in both his careers—Evan draws on his father's training about the power of the mind. "There is a place we all go to find belief or insight or courage, to transform our minds from fear or doubt to belief that we can do what we need to do. For me, whether it's acting, or being a doctor and saving someone's life, it is all about taking control of a reality and believing you can make something good happen."

In a sense, exercising willpower is almost ceremonial for Evan. "Ceremony definitely comes into it. It is about connecting to something—maybe yourself, maybe the Creator, maybe the larger world out there—and asking for the best instead of just going through the motions. For example, if I'm trying to help a sick child, I can confine my efforts to seeing them once or twice while they lie in a hospital bed, or I can do *everything* in my power to help this young person. It makes a huge difference whether you commit or don't. You can just be okay at what you do, or you can be the kind of person who says, 'Until the end of my days I will fight for the absolute best in myself and truly make a difference.' That's where ceremony comes in, making that request of your inner, higher self, or of the universe, to be the best person you can be and believing in the best of the world as well."

In his medical work, Evan is a firm believer in a holistic approach to working with Aboriginal people. "That approach is a very natural one for us. In an indigenous health system, you look at the whole person, not just the part they are complaining about. That's second nature." If a child has a sore stomach, for example, focusing on that single issue is a mistake: "That's treating the stomach ache, not the child. But the sore stomach may just be a symptom of something else going on. What's happening with that child that might be making them feel bad? You have to work to find out the answer to that question, if you really are going to do your best to protect that child from harm."

Cultural understanding is important as well. "Doctors need to understand that Aboriginal people may have different perspectives on what is important for health," Evan says. "If you ask them what makes them feel well, they probably won't say 'good health care.' They will mention ideas like opportunity, equality, culture, language, self-determination, beauty, hope and love. These may be very esoteric concepts to some, but because Aboriginal people have been denied them for so long, they have attained a vital importance in their lives. They are critical determinants of Aboriginal health, and vital to maximizing someone's well-being and ability to make their own choices and do well in life."

As a father, Evan is trying to pass on his beliefs and experiences to his own sons, as well as some of his father's teachings. "My dad always encouraged me to try lots of different things and to take risks, even if it might seem a bit dangerous. Being on the land, playing soccer, missing school to be with the old-timers—these all involve a little bit of risk. Most of the time it would work out fine, and sometimes it would work out spectacularly well. I think sometimes we forget that if we are willing to put ourselves out there, most of the time it will be good. I try to get my sons to think that way too."

All the same, things have changed since he was a youth. "I had to drive a boat in a storm when I was eight years old. I can't imagine my sons having that experience. We had to kill to eat. My sons, if they don't shoot anything, that's fine, they can go to the supermarket. Things are different now." Nonetheless, Evan is instilling in them good beliefs and practices and the ability to stick up for themselves, a quality he values highly. "My father always told me to be careful of not being naive. You have to be ready for people to want to hurt you and be resilient to it, and prepared to stand

Evan wins a Juno Award in 2011 for his performance co-hosting that year's National Aboriginal Achievement Awards on the Aboriginal Peoples Television Network with fellow actor Adam Beach.
Courtesy National Aboriginal Achievement Foundation, John Ecker photo

up for yourself. It is just a reality. You don't grow your kids up to be beautiful human beings without making certain that the first person they encounter who mocks them or says an unkind word won't be able to knock them down and destroy them."

As a gay Aboriginal man, Evan is anything but naive about how harsh other human beings can be. He was fortunate to have parents who would not tolerate homophobia. "My father said, 'No one is going to call you down in front of me!' That was his way of saying he wasn't embarrassed about me being gay." He wants his sons to be equally strong when they encounter homophobia or racism in their daily lives. "If someone can embarrass you by saying 'Your dad's gay,' or bring you down with a few simple words like, 'You're dumb,' or 'You're a stupid Indian,' then you're not very strong. You have to stand up to that. You have to say, 'What the hell do you know?' I have told them it's going to happen, and they need to be ready. Luckily, my boys have developed a good system of beliefs where they know not to take guff from others. If someone puts gay people down, they ask them not to say stupid things about their dad. If someone says something racist, they tell them they won't tolerate those stupid ideas about who Aboriginal people are."

In the meantime, Evan is walking his own talk, speaking at conferences and featuring in several documentaries about Aboriginal health and well-being, dedicating himself wholeheartedly to his medical practice, and teaching health sciences students many of the same things he is teaching his sons about the importance of cultural well-being. His actor side has not been neglected: *Doctor E,* part talk show and part documentary about health in First Nations communities, is scheduled to air on the Aboriginal Peoples Television Network in 2014. A Carlos Ferrand movie called *4U,* in which Evan plays "the nicest dad in the world, whose daughter is in a juvenile detention centre for robbery," is also scheduled to premiere in 2014, and Evan has a new script of his own in the works called *Stone Faces.*

He has never stopped learning from his father, whom he visits all the time. The television and video games get turned off, and his sons are told to gather around and listen to what their grandfather has to say. "Sometimes they don't appreciate that, having to subscribe to traditional ways instead of the modern. But I understand that. When I was a kid I used to feel sorry for myself that I had to go out on the land and fish and hunt and work, and sleep outside in all weathers, when it seemed all the other children got to play in their own yard or watch television and sleep in a nice warm bed. But now I thank god my dad didn't let me do that."

Both Evan and his father have a lot of hope invested in the boys, and indeed in all the young people following in their footsteps. "My dad was reminding us recently how doing things the old way, or the traditional way, isn't something you just make up along the way. You have to study it, and work hard at it. I am seeing more and more young people willing to do that, and excited about the old ways, starting to appreciate their value within themselves," he says.

"That gives me a great deal of hope for the future, that we will be seeing generations to come that are strong and are willing to work hard that way to achieve something good, or to help other people, or maybe just to get to a normal place. That would be just fine too. It's what we all need to keep doing."

Thoughts from Sophie Pierre

b. 1950
Recipient of the Order of British Columbia
Ktunaxa Nation
(interviewed in 2012)

St. Mary's Indian Band Council member, 1978–2008 (26 years as chief)
Diploma in business administration, Camosun College
Award-winning businesswoman and director
Former chair, First Nations Finance Authority
Chief commissioner, BC Treaty Commission, 2009–13
Grandmother and mentor

My mother, Malyan Michel, gave me a great foundation of strength as a young child. She instilled in me a really firm belief in who I am, who my people are and where we belong. Because of that, I was able to identify with my heritage. Wherever I go in this territory, I know my ancestors have been here before me. It makes me strong to know who I am.

I was very fortunate. As a small child, I also learned my language from my grandfather, who died when I was three, and from my great-aunt until the age of six. Neither of them spoke any English and I had to learn Ktunaxa if I wanted to speak with them. When you learn the language that young, it is a huge advantage. You never really forget it. It is simply part of who you are.

It's so important that young people have a foundation like that to build on, the same strength in knowing who they are. When I was a child, so

Photo courtesy BC Treaty Commission

222

many children didn't have what I had. Even though I was taken away to residential school from the time I was six until I was fifteen years old, I never suffered physical abuse there as so many others did. I retained my language and sense of identity. But so many other children were taken away completely from their families and homes and culture. They lost everything. We're all still paying the emotional and physical price for that.

The negative effects of losing contact with your cultural identity and your language are well documented. That's why we are putting so much effort now into education and learning the language and about the culture. It is an uphill struggle to get the mainstream school system to incorporate First Nations' language and culture into the curriculum and to embrace First Nations' models and perspectives, but there are some positive things happening, at least here in our territory.

My son works in the Southeast Kootenay School District and he's been given incredible latitude to introduce Ktunaxa history and cultural teachings into the local curriculum, which is just wonderful. My generation still has a hard time accepting looking at things differently, but children have very open minds. They are very receptive to hearing this kind of information and learning different perspectives. It really empowers not only our kids, but all the children in those classes to learn about who we are in British Columbia and our collective history together. That's a very good thing.

That's where the seeds of change get planted so that tomorrow's cultural landscape will look very different. Steps like this give me real confidence for the next generation, that maybe they will have a future free from discrimination and marginalization and full of self-confidence and success in life instead. That's going to be good for everyone too. I think the opportunities for my grandchildren are boundless. That's the generation we have been working so hard for, the kids going into elementary and high school now who will be taking their place in the footsteps of people like Beverley O'Neil[15] and Troy Sebastian,[16] who in turn came after the people in my generation.

We're all working to make sure these young people know there is a better world out there waiting for them. It's so important that they feel good about who they are. If they start from that solid foundation of self-awareness and pride, there are no limits on what they can do.

I look at the young people that I have mentored over the years, like

15 See "Aiming Past the Finish Line," page 131.
16 See "Only One Lifetime," page 181.

Sophie Pierre, centre, with her mother, Malyan Michel, right, and a young Beverley O'Neil (date uncertain). *Photo courtesy Beverley O'Neil / Sophie Pierre*

Beverley and others, people I have helped to build that foundation for themselves. I can see how well they have done in their lives and how their families thrive as well as a result. They feel good about who they are. None of them question whether they can or can't do something. They know they can do whatever they set out to do.

That's the teaching I gave them and I try to give to any of the young people I cross paths with—that they have what it takes to do whatever they want in life. We have brilliant young people in our Nations. They aren't just our future leaders; they're British Columbia's future leaders. It's very exciting to think about how much better it will be for all the children of tomorrow because of that.

Postscript
The Strength of Identity: Connections between Culture and Well-being

"Language is our birthright," Renée Sampson says softly. The thirty-year-old SENĆOŦEN language teacher from Tsartlip, north of Brentwood Bay on the Saanich Peninsula of southern Vancouver Island, has tears in her eyes as she speaks.

"Bⁿⁿut it was deliberately taken away from us by the residential schools. People should know that. That's why our young people don't know the language, and all our social problems stem from the disconnection of our young people to our culture because they don't know our language. Without that sense of cultural identity, they just don't know who they are. We have a right to get it back. We *deserve* to be who we are."

Renée is sitting with a group of other language apprentices and teachers in the SENĆOŦEN language room at the W̱SÁNEĆ (Saanich) Adult Education Centre at Tsartlip. Sunlight is sprawling through the windows over the colourful posters on the walls; cheerful preschoolers chattering in SENĆOŦEN can be heard from the room next door. But there is a sombre mood here as the group discusses the issue of language and cultural identity. Renée and her colleagues know all too well that British Columbia's remaining thirty-two indigenous languages are at serious risk of extinction. The 5 percent of First Nations people who are still fluent in those languages are mostly elders from a tiny pool of speakers that dwindles rapidly every year.

That's a very frightening situation to people like Renée and PENÁC (David Underwood), a University of Victoria arts graduate. "You could say that our language takes care of our people," PENÁC explains. "Our words tell us how to behave through the values that are inherently embedded in them. That's why it isn't easy to translate into English sometimes, because those values get lost in translation. That's why we need to know the original language."

Tell someone in English to gather some plants, and the words have an exact meaning: "Go pick some herbs." In SENĆOŦEN, the language that PENÁC speaks, the phrase would communicate a litany of other values and practices that must be carried out in the gathering of the plants—ecological, ceremonial, spiritual and community-related—and would take pages of English translation to capture, even supposing that were truly possible.

SELILIYE (Belinda Claxton), PENÁC's aunt, nods in agreement.

"SENĆOŦEN is not just a language, it's a philosophy," she explains. "Speaking the language is a way of being for us." Understanding that plants cannot be randomly or carelessly harvested is vital in a climate where regeneration can be slow, and where the resource must be shared with numerous others. Knowing how, when and where to gather the plants and having respect for the process and the values that those plants represent also sets a high standard for human behaviour. "That's why the language gives back to the young people a strong sense of who they are, and greater self-confidence in how they conduct themselves. That's why the thought of losing the language is so frightening."

Kendra Underwood, who is the director of the Saanich Adult Education Centre at the W̱SÁNEĆ School Board, adds: "I think that many people don't understand how important our language is in our lives. We deserve to have our language be healthy and

Kendra Underwood
Courtesy Peter Brand

whole. We need help for that to happen, because if we don't do it now, it will be too late. And it comes down to this: we *didn't* let it go. It was taken from us."

The story of the abuses that took place at residential schools is now well known. Less well known is that one of the goals of the schools was to exterminate Aboriginal languages by interrupting their transmission from generation to generation—and in the process of doing so, stamp out cultural world views that were in conflict with those of the colonizers. It was an effective strategy, according to Andrea Bear Nicholas, former chair of native studies at St. Thomas University in Fredericton, New Brunswick: "It took only two or three generations before people stopped using their language."

The loss of language intensified when child welfare services were put in the hands of provincial governments in the 1960s. Under what is now infamously known as the "Sixties Scoop," Aboriginal

Andrea Bear Nicholas
Courtesy St. Thomas University

children were taken in droves from their families and placed into non-Aboriginal foster homes far from home. More than half of them were sent to the United States and Europe, never to return.

It wasn't much easier for those who remained. When SELILIYE went to public school in the 1960s, she wasn't allowed to speak SENĆOŦEN, her mother tongue. "It was a nightmare for me," she recalls. "We were taught Latin instead. I had no idea what any of it meant. I would get called a dumb Indian. I dreaded going." Eventually, she simply stopped. "There was no point. I learned nothing at all."

SELILIYE, along with all the other children deprived of their languages, was the victim of a universally accepted truth: remove the language from the child, and the emotional, cultural and academic costs in terms of disproportionately high rates of unemployment, school dropouts, addictions, crime and suicide—let alone the consequential burden on medical, welfare and correctional systems—are enormous.

In 2007 Christopher Lalonde, who is now a psychology professor at the University of Victoria, co-wrote a report—starkly named *Aboriginal Language Knowledge and Youth Suicide*"—along with UBC psychology professor Michael J. Chandler and Darcy Hallett, now an assistant psychology professor at Memorial University.[17] The report described known socio-economic factors contributing to youth suicide rates in Aboriginal communities, such as poverty, and then overlaid an additional factor: absence of language.

Lalonde and his colleagues researched 150 communities in British Columbia, and discovered that language had more predictive power in anticipating suicide rates than any previously known indicator. Even more striking were these two facts: "Rates dropped to zero in communities in which at least half the members reported a conversational knowledge of their language," they wrote. In contrast, where there was little or no connection to language the suicide rate rose to *six* times higher than the national average.

That statistic bears repeating: in First Nations communities

17 See web.uvic.ca/~lalonde/manuscripts/2007CogDevt.pdf (accessed on May 20, 2013).

where the original language has effectively vanished, six times as many children are killing themselves as in other communities across the country where the kids are able to speak their mother tongue. In a country where youth suicide accounts for a quarter of all suicides, that means hundreds of First Nations children are dying at their own hands—and the link to a lack of connection to their culture is irrefutable. "Loss of language is the canary in the coalmine of cultural distress," the report's authors concluded. "The association between cultural collapse and the rise of public health problems is so uniform and so exceptionless as to be beyond serious doubt."

Underscoring what Renée, Kendra, PENÁC and others have said, the authors added that it is critical to understand that it is not the twenty-first-century social ills beleaguering many First Nations that have caused the loss of cultural connections to traditional values and languages. On the contrary, the finger must be squarely pointed at deliberate colonial strategies—such as the residential-school system—that were aimed at eradicating culture and language and that are directly responsible for this tragic state of affairs.

But things are changing. People like Renée Sampson are living proof that proactive language revitalization efforts are paying off in spades in terms of cultural well-being, especially for First Nations youth. At Thanksgiving a few years ago, Renée was present as her then sixteen-year-old niece led her cousins in performing a SENĆOŦEN drum song. "I was watching her," Renée recalls, "and thinking, here are these teenagers—they are at the point where they could be out drinking, dropping out of school, and getting pregnant—but they're not! They've embraced the language instead, and they're proud and they're healthy," she concludes happily.

It is now well established worldwide that children versed in their mother-tongue language, as well as the dominant cultural language, benefit from positive brain development and do well in all areas of education. Papua New Guinea has provided mother-

Renée Sampson
Courtesy Peter Brand

tongue education in indigenous languages since 1993. Andrea
Bear Nicholas says: "The results are striking. Children become
literate more quickly and learn English faster than children who
went through the old unilingual system, and score higher in all
subjects. The dropout rate has also decreased."

The same results have also emerged closer to home. Tracey
Herbert, executive director of the First Peoples' Cultural Council, notes the success of Mohawk and Cree immersion schools
founded in Ontario in the mid-1980s: "Their kids have higher high
school graduation rates than national averages, and some of the
highest rates of follow-through into post-secondary education of
any First Nations in Canada."

In British Columbia, the N'kmaplqs i Snma'mayat'tn klSqilxwet (Okanagan Indian Band Cultural Immersion School) is the
region's first school with Okanagan language and knowledge as its

foundation. Bill Cohen, PhD, a band councillor and former associate professor of indigenous studies at Okanagan University College, helped establish the K-7 school, now in its fifth year. "The community has two fundamental goals it wants to achieve with the school," he says. "They want the kids to be fluent in their language—to speak, think and dream in it. Equally importantly, they want the children to be successful in the provincial school curriculum and in gaining world knowledge. We're well on the way to meeting both those goals," he says with satisfaction.

Cohen says that most of the children going through the program shine when they enter high school, getting onto honour rolls, principals' lists and school sports teams. "There's a real difference in these kids," he observes. "They're more confident in public. They know who they are. They are healthy, happy young people who are succeeding in the public school system with ease." Kathy Michel, co-founder of the Chief Atahm immersion school in Chase, has had the same experience: "When my children entered the public school system at Grade 11, after being in the language immersion program, they opened up their science books and said, 'Oh, this is easy stuff. We were taught this way back in Grade 5.'"

Sl,OLTENOT (Madeline Bartleman) is another alumna of the W̱SÁNEĆ language apprenticeship program. A confident, articulate mother of four who studied for her bachelor of education degree at the University of Victoria, Sl,OLTENOT is living proof of the benefits of having grown up learning her language at the ȽÁU,WELṈEW̱ Tribal School at Tsartlip. "When I go out in the world," she says simply, "I know exactly who I am and where I come from, and I'm proud." Her children are now learning SENĆOŦEN at the same school. "The teachers say they are very fast learners and doing really well," she says proudly.

Mike Willie, who is thirty-six years old, is the cultural preservation and revitalization co-ordinator at the Gwa'sala-'Nakwaxda'xw K-7 School in Port Hardy, on northern Vancouver Island. Originally from Kingcome Inlet, Mike experienced both sides of the language coin growing up. "Because Kingcome Inlet is so isolated,

Mike Willie
Courtesy Mike Willie

we were able to retain our language and customs, even when they were banned by the government," he says. "I grew up hearing my language and singing the songs. It was wonderful."

That all changed when it was time for high school, however: after Grade 7, Kingcome Inlet families have to send their children away to complete high school. "I was sent to Victoria," Mike says. "I really struggled—it was a huge culture shock." Like SELILIYE, Mike wasn't taught about his own history: "I learned all about the Romans and the Vikings, but not about what happened right here in Canada to my people."

What saved him was the strong sense of identity that was ingrained in him from his earliest childhood. "I kept up my singing, even though I was far from home." Indeed, the remarkable teenager was so hungry to stay grounded in his culture that he skipped school regularly to spend time in the provincial government archives, transcribing tapes of his language. "The archivist thought I was researching for my degree in university, so he didn't question me being there!" Mike chuckles.

More sombrely, he reflects: "Having been taught in my language as a young child totally helped me with my self-confidence and getting through school and university. That's true of many kids from Kingcome—there is a really high success rate in post-secondary education and I attribute it directly to being grounded in the language." Take that away, and the results speak for themselves. "After all," he concludes, "if you don't know who you are, you're just roaming this world, lost. You're not grounded anywhere."

There is good work being done in the field by people like Bill Cohen and Kathy Michel, Saanich language guru STOLCEL (John Elliott), the First Peoples' Cultural Council and the University of Victoria. UVic is supporting young teachers like Renée and Mike by providing SENĆOŦEN teaching certification programs that are compatible with provincial school standards. The ŁÁU,WELṈEW̱ Tribal School, under STOLCEL's direction, supports two hundred K-9 students from the four Saanich First Nations communities with an extensive language curriculum. Pilot programs for pre-school "language nest" immersion programs around the province have also proved highly successful.

The First Peoples' Cultural Council runs a sophisticated web-based language archiving program called FirstVoices, in wide use by First Nations across British Columbia. The program was created more than a decade ago by STOLCEL, working with Peter Brand, who at the time was a teacher at the ŁÁU,WELṈEW̱ Tribal School (and who has since become the co-ordinator of the First-Voices program). STOLCEL's father, Dave Elliott, had created a SENĆOŦEN alphabet a few years previously. Peter stumbled across inexpensive software that made it possible to create a simple dictionary using Dave's alphabet, and FirstVoices was born.

In October 2010, a full audiovisual dictionary of SENĆOŦEN words and phrases became downloadable from iTunes, free of charge. This happened with the Halq'eméylem language too. These days the kids wandering around Tsartlip are, as often as not, busy checking out the dictionary on their smart phones. Their parents sneak a look whenever they can too. The possibilities in this digital world for connection and interconnection among First Nations people and their non-First Nations neighbours are endless.

Renée Sampson and PENÁĆ both hear stories that fill them with happiness: a child asking her mother in SENĆOŦEN if she is feeling all right; teenagers leaving giggly phone messages for each other in their language to foil their non-SENĆOŦEN-speaking parents, who smile indulgently and proudly behind their children's backs before heading quietly over to the W̱SÁNEĆ Adult Education Centre to enrol for adult language starter classes.

In 2010, SELILIYE graduated from Grade 12 at ŁÁU,WELṈEW̱ Tribal School, to which she had returned that year at the age of fifty-eight, courageously determined to finish school at last. It was a quiet ambition, but a meaningful one. No longer does she feel like a "dumb Indian"; she is now a proud and healthy W̱SÁNEĆ woman speaking her language. She is looking forward, with a heart full of tears and joy, to sitting at the kitchen table as she once did as a small child listening to her grandmother, but this time it is her grandchildren who will be speaking SENĆOŦEN.

"My achievements in life are totally attributable to knowing my language and my origins," Mike Willie says quietly. "Without that, I would be completely lost. Instead, I know exactly who I am."

Acknowledgements

This book has its origins in a conversation over lunch with A-in-chut, Assembly of First Nations National Chief Shawn Atleo.

Earlier in his political career, I'd profiled Shawn a couple of times in magazine stories, and we'd become friends over the years. When I first met him, I was immediately attracted by his clear-eyed vision of who he is and what he wants out of life. I was also awed by his energy. This was a busy guy.

Hereditary chief of the Ahousaht First Nation, co-chairman of the Nuu-chan-nulth Tribal Council, president of Umeek Human Resource Development Ltd., a Stanford grad and holder of an M.Ed., he had also found time to get married in between studying, and to co-produce two high-achieving teenagers (who have since become high-achieving adults who could also have been in this book—but, as I've already pointed out, where do I stop? For this book, one Atleo will just have to do).

That first interview, which took place in 2004 at the home that Shawn and his wife, Nancy, shared in north Nanaimo, was highly memorable. He was inspirational. He was sure of himself. He knew what he wanted out of life. He was also highly distracted by manic preparations going on in the background for son Tyson's high school prom in Nanaimo that night. Parental pride glowed out of every pore, even as he tried to answer my questions and ignore the constantly buzzing cellphone at his side. Nancy, who had picked me up from the Gabriola Island ferry dock, had talked non-stop all the way to their house about the logistics of managing both their son and their daughter, Tara, also still at high school, along with Shawn's crazy schedule.

That schedule would only get more intense as Shawn rose to national prominence and took on more responsibilities, among them the chancellorship of Vancouver Island University. Shawn never wavered in his devotion to his family, however. Tyson's prom night beat out a prime minister's meeting; matters of that

Shawn A-in-chut Atleo with Nancy, Tyson and Tara, 2010. *Courtesy Atleo Family*

importance were non-negotiable. It was a lot of fun to sit at their dining-room table and join in the swirl of conversation, offering an opinion on the blue tie or the stripes, the right time to collect Tyson's girlfriend, and whether or not little sister Tara would be permitted to make fun of Tyson while he was getting his picture taken in his prom-night finery.

Shawn's profile appeared alongside a number of others of several articulate, smart, self-assured First Nations men and women in the September 2004 issue of *BCBusiness* magazine, including Clarence Louie, Puuglas (Jody Wilson-Raybould), and Bonnie Leonard, and again in *Focus* magazine a year or so later, with Bruce Underwood, Adam Olsen and Bill Yoachim. All of these people talked about their lives, dreams, and hopes as Aboriginal Canadians in twenty-first-century British Columbia. They talked about having a foot in both worlds: the cultural world to which they are integrally linked as people of First Nations' heritage, and the other world in which they live their everyday lives just like anyone else. Their conversations opened a window of insight and understanding to their lives that challenged many of the stereotypes that non-Aboriginal Canadians often hold about First Nations people.

Two years later, over lunch that day, I idly commented to Shawn: "You know, there was so much positive reaction to all of your stories. Most people read nothing but bad press about First Nations, and yet there are so many Aboriginal Canadians doing great things. They're an inspiration to the young people, and they're a real wake-up call to everyone else stuck in a stereotype rut. Most of them seem to be just regular folks doing ordinary things, and some of them are doing extraordinary things, like you, but they're all interesting, wonderful people, with a very strong sense of their culture and its place in their lives.

"You all have this strong link to your cultural identity in common," I continued. "I've been thinking about doing a book telling your stories like this, about who you are, First Nations individuals living in twenty-first-century British Columbia, celebrating your culture and identity and just being people doing their best to live good, rewarding lives. I think a lot of people out there would be interested and inspired to read about people like you. What do you think?" Shawn, who has been working toward the goal of reconciliation for his people all of his adult life, put down his knife and fork and stared at me. He leaned over, grabbed me in a big hug and simply said: "Katherine, you *have* to write this book."

That was back in 2008. It took me a bit longer than I had originally planned, but here it is at last. I am proud, honoured and privileged to finally have presented *We Are Born with the Songs Inside Us,* and would like to thank the wonderful men and women who are in it, including Shawn, for entrusting their stories to me this way.

Apart from them, many other people also assisted and supported me in its completion. Thanks go to Grace Adams, Nancy Atleo, Michelle Benjamin, Peter Brand, Jennifer Brennan, Melody Charlie, Tanya Corbet, Courtney Daws, Brooke Finnigan, Sigrun Gilmour, Peter Holst, Brenna Latimer, Laura Leyshon, Sammy Jo Louie, Dave Mannix, Ashley Marston, Stephen May, Roberto

Nichelle, the Odjick family, Nancy Olding, Debra Powell, Matt Sheriko, Laura Uganecz, Richard Wagamese and Cherryl Williams for helping me with various matters, including scheduling interviews, obtaining photographs and permissions to use material, or just generally being great boosters. Cheryl Cohen was a sensitive, respectful and supportive editor who took great care with all of the stories in this book, and I am grateful to Howard White for recognizing the importance of publishing a book like this one.

My especial thanks to Cheryl Bryce (Lekwungen), Candace Campo (Sechelt), Michele Guerin (Musqueam), Maxine Tanner (Wet'suwet'en) and Bryan Williams (Ge-de-gilsxw), who all spent time with me during the conceptual stages of this book sharing their insights and thoughtful ideas about culture, identity and self.

My appreciation also goes to several organizations that contributed financial support to the writing of the book: the Association of British Columbia Land Surveyors, the Association of Canada Lands Surveyors, and Dockside Green, in Victoria.

My parents, Juliette and Michael Palmer, were—as they always have been—unwavering in their love and support as I went through all the usual highs and lows as this book slowly came into being. Caroline: thanks for being my proud big sister. Marc: thank you. You're the best (but you know that already).

Finally, I would like to acknowledge all the other people out there who could have been in this book and who all deserve to have their stories told and shared. Huy ch q'u, mussi, kleco, kleco, migwetch. Thank you!

—Katherine Palmer Gordon, June 2013

Photographs indicated in **bold**

Aboriginal Affairs and Northern
Development, 23, 140. *See also* Indian
and Northern Affairs, Department of.
Aboriginal Cultural Tourism
Authenticity Accreditation program,
140
Aboriginal Cultural Tourism Blueprint
Strategy, 140
*Aboriginal Language Knowledge and
Youth Suicide* (Lalonde et al.), 229–30
Aboriginal Opportunities Committee,
Vancouver Board of Trade, 101
Aboriginal Tourism Association of BC,
140
Adams, Evan Tlesla, 13, 45, 207–21, **209,
210, 215, 219**
Adams, Leslie, **210**–13, 220, 221
Adams, Mary Jane, **210,** 211, 213
Aglukkaq, Leona, 188
agreements, *see* treaties and agreements
Ahousaht First Nation, 159, 236
Alcheringa Gallery, 38
Alexander, Merle, 14, 145–58, **146, 149,
151, 154, 155**
Alexander, Stella, 146–47, **154,** 157
art
    Coast Salish, 36–37
    First Nations, 40
    See also Marston, John
Atleo, Nancy, 236, **237**
Atleo, Shawn A-in-chut, National Chief,
8–**9,** 13, 75, 77, 159, 236–**37,** 238
Atleo, Tara, **237**
Atleo, Tyson, 236–**37**

Baird, Edith, 109–10
Baird, Kim (Kwuntiltunaat), 13, 104–18,
105, 113, 115

Baird, Lorne, 109
Balangu, Teddy, 39, 41
Bartleman, Madeline, *see* Sl,OLTENOT
(Madeline Bartleman)
BC Treaty Commission, 222
Beach, Adam, 76
Bill C-31, 27, 110
Bitterly Divine, 91, 102
Bowcott, Sharon, 112
Brand, Peter, 234
British Columbia Achievement
Foundation, 14
British Columbia Creative Achievement
Award, 32
Bryce, Cheryl, 15, 239
Bull, Tommy, 71
Bure, Pavel, 61

Campbell, Peter, 39
Campo, Candace, 15, 239
Canadian Native Arts Fund, 45
Cassidy, Laura, **115**
Charlie, Melody, 175, 179
Charlie, Simon, 34, 36–38
Chief Atahm immersion school, 232
Child, Merv, 14
child and family services, and First
Nations, 128
Claxton, Belinda, *see* SELILIYE (Belinda
Claxton)
Cobalt, Anne-Marie, 36
Cohen, Bill, 232, 234
community planning, for First Nations,
50–51
control of one's life, importance of, 54
Coon, Silas, 36
Cowichan Tribes, 14
cultural identity, importance of, 103,
127–28, 141–42, 223

Delgamuukw v. British Columbia, 149, 153

Delorme, Ronnie, 75

Dennis, Robert, Chief Councillor, 167

Doctor E (TV show), 220

Dzawada̱'enux̱w First Nation, 14

Eaglequest Golf Club, 62

ecosystem management, 88

education

    First Nations culture and history in, 180, 223

    First Nations immersion schools, 231–32, 234

    pressure on First Nations students, 46, 157-58

    See also language, importance of

Elliott, Dave, 234

Elliott, John, *see* STOLCEL (John Elliott)

Ellis, Rob, 14

families, importance of, 79

First People's Cultural Council, 234

FirstVoices, 234

Fleming, Rob, 187

4U (film), 220

franchise, First Nations, 185–86

freedom, importance of, 162, 178–79

Gillis, Charlie, 15

Gitga'at (Hartley Bay), 16, 86, 89

Grant, Dorothy, 133

Guerin, Michele, 14, 239

Gwa'sala-'Nakwaxda'xw K-7 School, 232

Happynook, Tom Mexsis, 173

Headstart programs, 79

health care, *see* medicine

Herbert, Tracy, 231

Holbrook, Art, 39

Huu-ay-aht First Nations, 160—164, 166–67, 170, 173

Idle No More, 25, 77, 156

Indian Act, 27, 43, 50, 107, 118, 125–26, 162, 172–173, 177, 185

Indian and Northern Affairs, Department of, 23, 140,172, 177. *See also* Aboriginal Affairs and Northern Development

Indian Residential Schools Settlement Agreement, 48

Innu Nation, 150

Jacob, Gibby, Chief, 98, 99

Jacobs, Krisandra, 96

James, Carole, 187

Joe, Harry, Chief, 108

Jones, Tina, 82, **84,** 89

Joseph, Tewanee, 91–102, **93, 99, 100**

Kahtou, 140

Karpes, Shawn, 36

Ka:'yu:'k't'h'/ Che:k'tles7et'h First Nations, 170

Killer Whale and Crocodile (film), 40

Kitasoo/Xai'xais Nation, 16, 80, 83, 145–146, 157

Kitigan Zibi Anishinabeg First Nation, 55–56

Ktunaxa Nation Council, 131, 134–38, 181, 184, 191–93, 222

Kw'umut Lelum, 121, 127

Lachance, Steeve, 113, 114

Lalonde, Christopher, 229

language, importance of, 191, 222, 225–35

LaRue, Charlene, 76

law, as professional choice, 14

Lax Kw'alaams, high school band from, 15
Leech, Bernice, 70
Leech, Peter, 8, 64, 65–78, **67, 68, 72**
Leech, Walter, 70, 71, **72,** 72–73
legal decisions, and First Nations, 137, 153–55. See also *Delgamuukw v. British Columbia*
Lekwungen (Songhees Nation), 15
Leonard, Bonnie, 180, 237
Louie, Clarence, 103, 155, 237

ŁÁU,WELNEW Tribal School, 232, 234–235

Maa-nulth First Nations, 170–73, **171**
Manuel, George, Grand Chief, 73–74, **75,** 77–78
Marston, David, 34
Marston, Jane, 34
Marston, John, (Qap'u'luq) 30–41, **31, 33, 35, 38**
Marston, Luke, 36
Mathias, Joe, Chief, 94
medicine
    First Nations approach to, 46, 217–18
    cultural understanding and, 218
    studying from First Nations perspective, 46–47, 53
Mercer, Art, 14
Michel, Kathy, 232, 234
Michel, Malyan, 222, **224**
Monds, Elaine, 38–39
Moses, Jim, 20
Moses, Margaret, 22, 27, **28**
Moses, Ruby, 20, 22
Musqueam First Nation, 14, 61–62
Musqueam Golf and Learning Academy, 62

Nagoya Protocol, 152
National Aboriginal Achievement Foundation, 45
National Aboriginal Women in Leadership Distinction Award, 116
National Centre for First Nations Governance, 14
National Indian Brotherhood, 73
Native Courtworker and Counselling Association of British Columbia, 183
NDP, BC, 187–88
Neasloss, Doug, Chief, 16
Neville, John, 10–11
Nicholas, Andrea Bear, **228,** 231
Nicholas, Toby, 137–38
9/11, and border crossing, 43
Nisga'a Nation, 14, 15, 111, 171
N'kmaplqs i Snma'mayat'tn klSqilxwet (Okanagan Indian Band Cultural Immersion School), 231–32
Nuu-chah-nulth Tribal Council, 236

Odjick, Gino, 13, 55–64, **57, 58, 63,** 67, **68,** 76–77
Odjick, Gisele, 59
Odjick, Joe, 59–60
Okanagan Indian Band Cultural Immersion School (N'kmaplqs i Snma'mayat'tn klSqilxwet), 231–32
Olding, Tamara, 153, **155,** 157
Olsen, Adam, 206, 237
O'Neil, Beverley, 131–44, **133, 135, 143, 224,** 223
Osoyoos Indian Band, 103

Palembei Sunset (art), 41
Patrick, Archie, 48–49, **49**
Patrick, Lyana, 42–53, **44**
Patton, **21**
Paull, Andy, **97**

Paull, Percy, 95
Pauquachin First Nation, 79
PENÁC (David Underwood), 226, 235
Penticton Indian Band, 201
Peters, Agnes, 66–67
Phillips, Marisa, 14
Pierre, Sophie, 136, 140, **222–24**
Pockiak, Lori, 129
political system, and First Nations, 188
Porphyra (seaweed), 87–88
Powell, Debra, 196, 204
Price, Carey, 14
Puuglas (Jody Wilson-Raybould), 54, 237

Qap'u'luq (John Marston), 30, **31**
Qat'muk Declaration, 192

racism, systemic, 190
reconciliation
    basis for, 8, 188–90
    importance of, 159, 186
    See also treaties and agreements;
       Truth and Reconciliation
       Commission
residential schools
    compensation process, 198–99, 205
    language and, 228
    meaning of for First Nations, 199–200
    settlement agreement, 48
    vs. child and family services, 128
       See also Truth and Reconciliation
       Commission
Robinson, Elsie, 8
Robinson, Marven, 16

Sampson, Renée, 225–26, 230, **231**, 235
Sandercock, Leonie, 50
seafood, traditional, 88
Sebastian, John, 186
Sebastian, J.R., 186

Sebastian, Kenny, 186
Sebastian, Mark, 183, 184, 185, 186
Sebastian, Patricia, 183–84, **185**
Sebastian, Troy, 181–93, **182, 185, 192,**
    223
Secwepemc Nation, 73
self-control, importance of, 212
self-government, importance of, 107,
    159, 162
SELILIYE (Belinda Claxton), 226–27,
    229, 235
SENĆOŦEN, 226–27, 234–35
Sechelt, 15
Shuswap Nation, 180
Six Nations, 17, 20
Sixties Scoop, 228–29
Sliammon First Nation, 45, 207
Sl,OLTENOT (Madeline Bartleman), 232
Smoke Signals (film), 45, 214, 216
Snuneymuxw First Nation, 16, 121, **126,**
    128–29
Squamish First Nation, 91, 94–95, 96, 97
St'at'imc Nation, 65
Stellat'en First Nation, 42
stereotyping
    checklist, for "genuine Indian," 23
    dealing with, 19–20, 190
    for a young woman, 138–39
Stewart, Nikki, 15
STOLCEL (John Elliott), 234
Stz'uminus (Chemainus) First Nation,
    194
St. Mary's Indian Band, 134–136, 183,
    222
suicide, and language, 229–30
Sumas First Nation, 63
Sylvester, Tyrone, 14

Tanner, Maxine, 15, 239

Tenning, Anne, 194–205, **195, 199, 202, 205**

Tenning, Elizabeth, 197–99, 205

Tenning, Kathy, 200

The Fourth World: An Indian Reality (Manuel and Posluns), 73

therapeutic planning, 51

Thomas, Teyem, 16

T'it'q'et Village, 65, 70

Tk'emlups First Nation, 180

Toquaht Nation, 170

Touchie, Bernice, 178–179

Touchie, Evan, 174–79, **175, 178**

Touchie, Tyson, 178

Travels Across the Medicine Line (film), 43

treaties and agreements

  Evan Touchie on, 176–79

  history of, in BC, 171–72

  Huu-ay-aht First Nation, 162, 166–67, 170–73

  Jay Treaty (Treaty of London), 43

  Maa-nulth Treaty, 98, 170–73, **171,** 176

  Nisga'a First Nation, 111, 171

  Snuneymuxw First Nation, **126,** 128–29

  Squamish First Nation, 96

  Troy Sebastian on, 190–91

  Tsawwassen First Nation, 107–9, 111–12, 114, **115,** 116, 118–20

Tr'ondëk Hwëchin, 15

Trudeau, Pierre, 54, 73, 74

Truth and Reconciliation Commission, 11, 48

Tsartlip First Nation, 206, 225–226

Tsawwassen First Nation, 63, 104, 106–9, 111–12, 118–20

Tsawwassen reserve, 106–7

Tsimshian First Nations, 80, 87, 89

2010 Olympic and Paralympic Winter Games, 32, 91, 98–101, 140

Uchucklesaht Tribe, 170

Ucluelet First Nation, *see* Yuułuʔiłʔatḥ/ Ucluelet First Nation

Ulkatcho First Nation, 14

UN Declaration on the Rights of Indigenous Peoples, 73, 151–52

Underwood, Bruce, Chief, 79, 237

Underwood, David, *see* PENÁC (David Underwood)

Underwood, Kendra, **227**–28

Union of British Columbia Indian Chiefs, 73

Wagamese, Richard, 195–97, **196,** 204

War in the Woods, 147

Warner, Trudy Lynn, 160–70, **161, 168**

Webster, Daniel, 22, 27, **28**

Webster-Gibson, Lisa, 17–29, **18, 24**

Welcome Figure (art), 34, **35**

Wet'suwet'en First Nation, 15

We Wai Kai Nation (Cape Mudge), 54

Wheel of Fear, 67–69

White, Douglas, III, (Kwulasultun), Chief, 14, **126**

White, Gloria, 83, **85**

White, Joyce, 123

White, Lois Georgina, 83

White, Penny, 80–90, **81, 84**

White, Rae-Ann, 98, **99**

White, Willard, 83, **85**

White Light (art), 32, **33**

White Paper (1969), 73

Williams, Bill, Chief, 97

Williams, Bryan, 237

Williams, Remo, 120

Willie, Mike, 232–34, **233,** 235

Wilson, Bill, 54

Wilson-Raybould, Jody, *see* Puuglas (Jody
    Wilson-Raybould)
women, First Nations, 124, 184
World Council of Indigenous Peoples, 73
W̱SÁNEĆ, 226–227, 232, 235

Yinka Déné Language Institute, 49
Yoachim, Ivy, 122, 124, 130
Yoachim, Terri, 122
Yoachim, William "Bill," (Sqwulutsutun),
    121–30, **122, 126**, 237
Young, Wayne, 36
youth, First Nations, 64, 67 69, 77, 125,
    128, 180, 223–24, 230. *See also* Idle
    No More
Yuułuʔiłʔatḥ/Ucluelet First Nation, 170,
    174—179

About the Author

We Are Born with the Songs Inside Us is Katherine Palmer Gordon's sixth book. Under the name Katherine Gordon, she has also written *A Curious Life: The Biography of Princess Peggy Abkhazi* (2002); *The Slocan: Portrait of a Valley* (2004), which was shortlisted for the Hubert Evans Non-Fiction Prize, one of the BC Book Prizes, in 2005; *Made to Measure: A History of Land Surveying in British Columbia* (2006), winner of another BC Book Prize, the 2007 Roderick Haig-Brown Prize; *The Garden That You Are,* an exploration of the culture of gardeners (2007); and *Maps, Mountains and Mosquitoes: The McElhanney Story* (2010), winner of the silver medal for best corporate history in the 2011 Axiom International Business Book Awards.

A freelance journalist, she has also contributed to the *Globe and Mail* and *Vancouver Sun* newspapers, and *Canadian Geographic, BCBusiness, British Columbia* magazine, *GardenWise* and *Canadian Homes & Cottages,* among other publications.

She is a globe-trotting half-French, half-English expatriate Kiwi and a former lawyer who now lives on Gabriola Island, British Columbia, where she writes, gardens and works to support First Nations' rights and reconciliation.

Gary McKinstry photo